knit happy
with
Self-Striping Yarn

Bright, Fun and Colorful
Sweaters and Accessories
Made Easy

Stephanie Lotven
Creator of Tellybean Knits

PAGE STREET
PUBLISHING CO.

PAGE STREET
PUBLISHING CO.

Copyright © 2020 Stephanie Lotven

First published in 2020 by

Page Street Publishing Co.

27 Congress Street, Suite 105

Salem, MA 01970

www.pagestreetpublishing.com

Distributed by Macmillan, sales in Canada by The Canadian Manda Group.

24 23 22 21 20   1 2 3 4 5

ISBN-13: 978-1-64567-182-4

ISBN-10: 1-64567-182-8

Library of Congress Control Number: 2019957335

Cover and book design by Laura Benton for Page Street Publishing Co.

Photography by Samson Lotven & Stephanie Lotven

Printed and bound in the United States

For Grandma Gyte, who is always willing to share her love, strength and unconditional knitting support.

and for my mom, who promised she would learn to knit if I wrote a knitting book. Guess what, Mom!? I've got knitting needles, and I'm coming for you!

contents

Introduction

On May 17, 2016, I finished knitting the world's coolest socks. In case you are wondering how I could possibly remember the date, keep in mind that it was a big day for my feet. For three days I had been knitting the most beautiful self-striping socks. Propped up on my ottoman, my feet had been watching carefully. My tootsies had never seen such incredible socks—yellow, red, gray and blue with speckles and thick stripes and thin stripes, all knit out of merino wool and nylon. Even before my feet had a chance to wear those socks, they did a little dance. When I bound off the last cuff, it was a happy day. I popped my toes into my new favorite socks, skipped down the stairs, put on my shoes and just like that, my beautiful socks disappeared. They were gone. My poor feet were hidden, socks and all, inside my sneakers. Right then, looking down at my feet, I had an idea that would change the way I use my knitting stash.

A few months later, I released a knitting pattern called Sock Arms that was specifically designed to showcase self-striping yarn on sweater sleeves. Sock Arms was born from a simple idea: Self-striping yarn is just too thrilling to be hidden away in your shoes. Sorry, feet!

If you are new to self-striping yarn, then let me tell you a secret. It is magnificent! Each skein contains its own little rainbow of possibility—a whole palette of colors you didn't have to choose, because the dyer already did it for you! Somehow, knitting with self-striping yarn makes every project seem faster. Soon you will give up the usual knitter's mantra of "one more row" in favor of "one more stripe." And when you do bind off, you will have a project with almost no ends to weave in!

Perhaps you are not at all new to self-striping yarn. Maybe, like me, you have spent many hours knitting incredible socks out of incredible self-striping yarn. You already know that self-striping yarn is magnificent, but now you want to find new ways to use it. Let me help you. In these pages, you will find patterns to showcase your precious rainbow skeins on your neck, your head, your hands and your sleeves! No more hiding your brightest rainbow yarn under your pant legs. Let's liberate your yarn!

In this book, I will show you how to plan small, relaxing knits as well as bigger, more ambitious projects for your stripes. Together we will play with simple techniques and strategies that will make every stripe shine. Sprinkled into every page of this book, I will share the tricks I've learned from years of knitting, ripping, wearing and designing with self-striping yarn so that you don't have to struggle to get beautiful results. I've included step-by-step tutorials, specialized tips and clear instructions to help you knit fuss-free, stunning garments and accessories. Let me show you how to use stripes in your knitting so that they flatter your body and invigorate your wardrobe. Soon you'll be flying from stripe to stripe wondering why you kept those incredible skeins locked away in your shoes for so long.

Go grab your yarn. It's time to knit a rainbow.

Stephanie Lotven

About the Skill Levels

Beginner

These patterns are appropriate for new knitters. They use knits and purls. There may be simple shaping using increases and decreases.

- Indicator Shawl (page 97)
- Wave at the Rainbow Cowl (page 77)

Adventurous Beginner

These patterns use repetitive stitch patterns, basic shaping and/or basic colorwork. Increases and decreases, bind offs and cast ons may be used for shaping. No short rows are used for shaping.

- Backdrop Hat (page 63)
- Encompassing Cowl (page 87)
- Flipped Shawlette (page 123)
- Gallivant Hat (page 69)
- Parallel Currents Mittens (page 17)
- Rainbow Adventure Fingerless Mitts (page 29)
- Rainbow Blowout Cowl (page 91)
- Rapid Run Hat (page 47)
- Slippery Cowl (page 81)

Intermediate

These patterns include cables, more complicated stitch patterns and more involved colorwork and finishing methods. Short rows may be used for shaping.

- Backlit Tee (page 171)
- Bright Axis Tee (page 155)
- Daring Double Shawl (page 115)
- Drop a Rainbow Pullover (page 161)
- Everyday Magic Bonnet (page 55)
- For the Thrill Shawl (page 101)
- Glitz Mittens (page 39)
- Leapfrog Mittens (page 33)
- Little Sock Arms Cardigan (page 139)
- Onward & Outward Shawl (page 109)
- Showered in Rainbows Baby Sweater (page 147)
- Sidelong Glance Hat (page 51)
- Sock Arms Cardigan (page 129)

Advanced

These projects have the highest level of complexity. Expect to find patterns with complex colorwork, intricate short rows and specialty finishing methods. These projects are skill-heavy and include multiple referrals to special techniques.

- Sharp Curve Mittens (page 21)

Getting Started

What Is Self-Striping Yarn?

Self-striping yarn is dyed to create stripes at set intervals as you knit.

There are two types of self-striping yarn that you will see in this book:

Self-striping yarn with clearly defined stripes. The stripes knit from this yarn will be obvious and graphic. When one color ends, the next begins. The Leapfrog Mittens (page 33) and the Sidelong Glance Hat (page 51) show examples of this type of self-striping yarn.

Self-striping yarn with a gradient. The stripes in this yarn will slowly transition from one color to the next, but there is still obvious striping. The Wave at the Rainbow Cowl (page 77) and the Drop a Rainbow Pullover (page 161) show examples of this type of self-striping yarn.

Narrow Stripes Versus Wide Stripes & Everything in Between

The size of a stripe knit with self-striping yarn is not universal. Yarns vary from brand to brand and colorway to colorway, so it is important to get to know your stripes before you choose a project.

The shorter the length of yarn in each color, the narrower the knitted stripes will be. The longer the length of yarn in each color, the wider the knitted stripes will be. The width of the stripe will be important when planning your project. Narrow stripes are best for patterns with small circumferences or fewer stitches per round/row. Mittens, for example, are a great project for narrow stripes. You will also find that several of the shawls, such as the For the Thrill Shawl (page 101) and the Daring Double Shawl (page 115), are great projects for narrow stripes. Wider stripes are ideal for projects with a larger circumference or width. The Indicator Shawl (page 97) or the Backlit Tee (page 171) are particularly fun projects for yarns with thick stripes.

The best way to decide if your yarn is right for a particular project is to swatch it.

Swatching

Knitters always hate to hear this, but swatching is important. You should do it. It will save your life! Okay, probably not your life, but it can certainly save your knitting project.

A swatch will give you essential insight into your yarn before you invest hours of work in a knitting project. Swatching will help you knit a garment that actually fits, avoid yarn chicken and inform you about the drape of the fabric your yarn can produce. When you swatch a self-striping yarn, you will gain another vital piece of information that will help you prepare for your project: how it will stripe.

Sleeves, hats, mittens, shawls and cowls are all worked with a different number of stitches. If you change the number of stitches, you change the size of the stripe. The more stitches you have in a row/round, the narrower the stripe will be. The fewer stitches you have in a row/round, the wider the stripe will be. The gauge will also change the way a yarn stripes. A larger gauge will use more yarn per stitch, making the stripe narrower. A smaller gauge will use less yarn per stitch, making the stripe wider. This is why you need to swatch! You simply won't know what your self-striping yarn is capable of until you knit a swatch for your project AT GAUGE. So, let's get swatching!

Step 1: Knit your swatch.

Knit your swatch just as you normally would when preparing for a new project. When you are finished swatching, blocking and drying your swatch, check to make sure that you have achieved the gauge specified in the pattern (see photo 1 on next page).

> TIP: Unless the color repeat is quite long, I like to knit every color in the sequence at least once, so that I have a clear sense of the colors and the order of the colors in the yarn.

Step 2: Choose the narrowest stripe.

In some self-striping yarns, the stripes will all be the same size. In other yarns, the size of the stripes will vary. If the stripes are different sizes, choose the stripe that is the narrowest in the color sequence. If all the stripes are the same width, choose any stripe.

Step 3: Count your stitches.

Now, count all the stitches in your chosen stripe, and make a note of that number. This number tells you how many stitches you can knit in a single color of your self-striping yarn in order to create one complete row/round at gauge.

> TIP: Do not count the stitches in the first stripe of your swatch. Cast-on stitches use more yarn than a typical stitch and will make your stitch count per stripe less accurate.

Step 4: Check the pattern.

Once you know the maximum number of stitches you can knit in a single color of your self-striping yarn, you can decide if it is right for your project. At the beginning of every pattern in this book, the "Maximum Stitches Used for a Self-Striping Row/Round" section will tell you the largest number of stitches you can expect to knit in that pattern using self-striping yarn, according to your size.

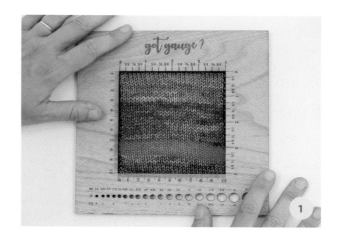

Step 5: Assess your stripe.

When I am knitting in self-striping yarn, my goal is to be able to work at least one complete ROUND or two complete ROWS in every color of the self-striping yarn. If your yarn is not able to achieve one complete round or two complete rows, the stripes might not look like stripes at all. A single color could fail to connect with itself and then the yarn may pool or look more like a variegated yarn.

Let me give you an example of how you will use this information for the patterns in this book. Let's say I am preparing to knit the Rapid Run Hat (page 47) in an adult size large. I have swatched my self-striping yarn, and I have achieved the appropriate gauge for the pattern. I have decided to count all the stitches in a single pink stripe, because it is my narrowest stripe, and find that I have 170 stitches in that stripe.

For my size, the pattern states that the maximum stitches used for a self-striping round is 80 stitches. I then divide 170 stitches by 80, which equals 2.1. This means that I can work just over two complete rounds in pink. This yarn is a good choice for an adult size large Rapid Run Hat. High five!

Color Repeat

A color repeat is the specific set of colors that occur over and over again in the same order in your yarn.

For example, if you are knitting a yarn with four colors that repeat in the same sequence—pink, blue, gray, purple, for example—then those four colors are your color repeat. If you are knitting a yarn with two colors that repeat— brown and white, for example—then those two colors are your color repeat.

Swatching your yarn is a great way to see and understand the color repeat before you jump into your project. If your dyer doesn't have a photo of the complete color repeat, consider winding your yarn slowly into a ball so that you can make note of the order of colors. Do not assume that the color repeat will be limited to a small series of stripes. Self-striping dyers are creative and ambitious

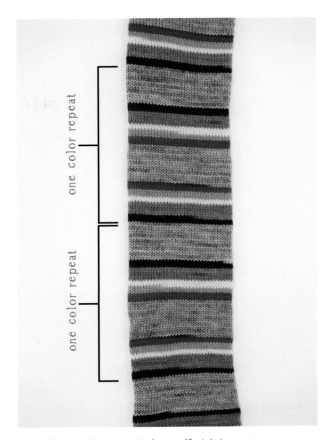

one color repeat

one color repeat

Identifying color repeats in a self-striping yarn.

color experts, and long, complex color repeats have been gaining popularity among dyers and knitters. Need a fun example? Check out the 40-stripe color repeat in the Slippery Cowl (page 81).

Finally, keep in mind that the order of your colors will change depending on which end of the skein you use to begin your project. If you pull the yarn from one end of the skein, the color repeat will be ordered one way, but if you begin from the other end of the skein, the order will be reversed.

Combining Colors

Knitters often complain that it is difficult to put colors together when planning a knitting project. I wholeheartedly agree. Color choices are difficult—that is, unless you are working with self-striping yarn. Then, putting together colors is easy and downright deliriously fun because you can cheat. When you buy a skein of self-striping yarn, you are purchasing another person's color knowledge. That skein of yarn might contain everything that a dyer knows about blue, or all the best colors to knit with pink. Each skein is packed full of color theory, and it is already done for you. All you need to do is steal a bit of that color knowledge and use it to your advantage.

Throughout this book, you will find lots of color inspiration. I invite you to dive right into the patterns, using the color combinations and yarns that I have chosen for each pattern. However, if you would prefer to make your own color choices and use some yarn that's already in your stash, here are three simple ways to choose solid yarns to accompany your self-striping yarn.

Option One

Choose a color that is already in the striping pattern. This is always a safe bet, because you know it will coordinate with the self-striping yarn. If you are knitting a project that calls for a solid yarn to accompany your self-striping, pick your favorite color from the color repeat and use it as your accompanying solid color. For example, if you

are knitting with a self-striping yarn that has purple, blue, black and orange in the stripes, simply choose one of these colors, like blue. You can see this strategy in action in the Onward & Outward Shawl (page 109).

> TIP: Pairing a self-striping yarn with a solid yarn that matches one of the stripe colors will make those stripes POP when you knit them together.

Option Two

Choose a neutral. If you have a particularly vibrant self-striping yarn, or you are uncertain about which color you want to highlight, consider pairing your self-striping yarn with white, gray or black. Neutral yarn is like a great pair of jeans. It goes with everything and detracts from nothing. Neutrals will let the self-striping pattern shine without looking strange or unflattering. You can see an example of this pairing in the Sock Arms Cardigan (page 129).

> TIP: If you pair a self-striping yarn with white yarn, make sure to swatch and wet block your self-striping and white yarn together before you jump into the project. With so much color in a skein of self-striping yarn, you need to make sure that none of the colors will bleed onto the white when washed.

3

TIP: If you are pairing a self-striping yarn and a solid yarn for stranded colorwork, I recommend using option three. In order to create the most graphic colorwork possible, there should be absolutely no overlap in the colors of the self-striping yarn and the contrasting yarn. So, if your self-striping yarn contains yellow, pink and blue, then your contrasting yarn should not have any yellow, pink or blue in it. Overlapping colors will muddy the colorwork motif, making it more difficult to see. Using option three will always keep your colorwork crisp and tidy. See the Glitz Mittens (page 39) for an example of option three used in stranded colorwork.

Option Three

Choose a color you love that is NOT in the striping pattern at all. This is the trickiest of the three color combining options. Essentially, you are choosing a color that you think will improve or complement the colors that are already in the self-striping yarn. The simplest way to do this is to choose a color that is in the same color family as one or more of the colors in the self-striping yarn. For example, if the self-striping yarn contains blues and purples, you can choose another cool color, like green. If the self-striping yarn contains pinks and reds, consider choosing a warm color, like orange. Option three will require some experimentation, and I highly recommend swatching your entire color repeat with your chosen solid. You can see an example of yarns paired using this option in the Backdrop Hat (page 63).

Special Magical Options

You may decide that you would like to pair a self-striping yarn with a speckled or variegated yarn. I support you! Speckles and variegation can add extra depth of color to your project. When I pair self-striping with speckled or variegated yarns, I like to use yarns that are lightly speckled or lightly variegated, because they are not as visually busy. Since self-striping yarns are already full of visual interest, a highly speckled or highly variegated yarn may overwhelm your project. Choose a yarn that contains some of the colors in the self-striping yarn. For example, if your self-striping yarn contains green, yellow and orange, consider pairing it with a gray yarn with green speckles. You can see an example of how I paired speckled yarn with self-striping yarn in the For the Thrill Shawl (page 101).

Colorful
mittens
with Room to Play

When you knit striped mittens, you get to take a little break from the knitting rules. Grab your yarn, experiment and play. With rainbow mittens, you can go wild, because mittens, my dear friend, are a knitter's playground. If you are new to self-striping yarn, mittens are the perfect place to start. The mittens in this chapter are not your ordinary mittens. These out-of-the-box constructions will have you giggling with glee as you rethink a thumb gusset, find a whole new way to shape a mitten top and draw surprising lines with your stripes. Small projects are great for learning what your yarn is capable of, because you don't need much yardage or time to try out a new trick. No need to invest weeks and hundreds of dollars in a sweater to see what short rows do to stripes (it's awesome, btw). Instead, grab a single skein of yarn and spend a happy afternoon knitting up Leapfrog Mittens (page 33).

In these pages, we will experiment with techniques you don't typically get to use in mittens, so that you are prepared for bigger, more ambitious projects in the chapters to come. We will reimagine common knitting techniques, like stranded colorwork in the Glitz Mittens (page 39), so that you don't just expect your stripes to stripe. You may not know it yet, but your yarn can do so much more than just make straight lines.

The mittens and fingerless mitts in this chapter were designed to break the rules. Forget your mitten expectations and join me for some truly playful knitting. Try out a nontraditional thumb gusset in the Rainbow Adventure Fingerless Mitts (page 29) or warp the palm of your mittens with simple increases and decreases in the Parallel Currents Mittens (page 17). Ready for some real playtime? Cast on the center-out Sharp Curve Mittens (page 21) and enjoy a pattern that is pure fun—no swing set required.

Parallel Currents Mittens

Skill Level: Adventurous Beginner

When I was a kid, my sister and I would take our little inflatable inner tubes to the creek. We'd plop ourselves into the tubes and ride the current side by side until my mom called for us to come back upstream. Those simple days on the water inspired these delightful, carefree mittens. Increases and decreases are one of the easiest ways to play with the direction of the stripes in your knitting. By placing increases on the front and back of the hand and decreases on the sides of the hand, the stripes bend to create a playful current of color that is both uncomplicated to knit and graphically striking. As a bonus, there is no extra shaping to work at the top of the mitten, because the increases create a point that naturally forms to fit the tips of your fingers. So hop on and ride the current with these happy mittens.

Construction

Each mitten is knit seamlessly in the round from the bottom up. The thumb gusset is created using simple increases. The thumb stitches are then placed on hold while the palm is completed. The top of the mitten is joined with the Kitchener Stitch method (see page 181). Finally, the thumb stitches are placed back on the needles and joined and worked in the round.

Maximum Stitches Used for a Self-Striping Round: 53 (59, 75, 81, 85, 89)

Sizes

Toddler (Child, Adult S, Adult M, Adult L, Adult XL)

See the Finished Measurements on page 18 to choose your size.

NOTE: To find your size, determine the circumference of your hand, excluding the thumb, by wrapping a flexible tape measure around the knuckles of your hand. Choose a size approximately 0.5 inches (1.25 cm) smaller than your hand circumference.

Yarn

- Fingering weight yarn, Nomadic Yarns Trusty Sock
- (75% superwash merino and 25% nylon, 462 yards / 3.5 ounces [422.5 m / 100 g])
- Sample shown in "Astronomy Tower"
- 1 skein
- 125 (150, 165, 175, 190, 210) yards / [114 (137, 151, 160, 174, 192) m]

Yarn Notes

I knit these mittens using one of my favorite sock yarns. Durable, soft and graphic, this yarn is incredibly fun to knit!

Needles

US 3 (3.25 mm) and US 2 (2.75 mm) DPNs or needles for small circumference knitting, or as required to meet gauge

Gauge

28 stitches and 40 rows = 4 inches (10 cm) in stockinette stitch on LARGER needles, in the round after blocking

NOTE ON GAUGE: I have provided the plain stockinette gauge for this pattern because it is the easiest stitch to swatch in preparation for your mittens. However, you will find that the increases and decreases that create the chevron shaping in this pattern warp the stockinette. This is why the palm circumference is smaller than you would expect based on the number of stitches you cast on.

Notions

- Tape measure
- 5 stitch markers
- Scissors
- Scrap yarn
- Tapestry needle

Finished Measurements

Sample shown is Adult S.

A. **Palm Circumference:** 4.75 (5.25, 6.5, 7, 7.5, 8) inches / [12 (13.5, 16.5, 18, 19, 20.5) cm]

B. **Palm Length:** 5 (6.5, 7.75, 8.25, 8.5, 9) inches / [13 (16.5, 19.5, 21, 21.5. 23) cm]

C. **Cuff Length:** 1.25 (1.5, 2, 2, 2, 2) inches / [3 (4, 5, 5, 5, 5) cm]

D. **Total Length:** 6.25 (8, 9.75, 10.25, 10.5, 11) inches / [16 (20.5, 25, 26, 26.5, 28) cm]

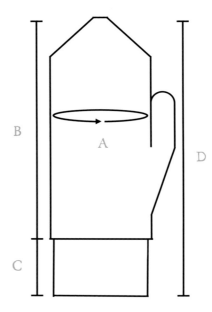

Abbreviations	
BOR	beginning of round
CO	cast on
dec	decrease
DPNs	double pointed needles
inc	increase
k	knit
k2tog	knit two together
m	marker
m1L	make one left
m1R	make one right
p	purl
pm	place marker
rep	repeat
sl	slip
sm	slip marker
ssk	slip, slip, knit
st(s)	stitch(es)

Pattern

Both mittens are knit identically.

> Note: When using a self-striping yarn, on the first round of each new color, knit all the purl sts in that round. Substituting a knit st for a purl st in the color change rounds will give you a clean color transition. When you have completed the first round of the new color, continue to work the purl sts according to the pattern.

Cuff

Using SMALLER needles, CO 40 (44, 56, 60, 64, 68) sts. Place a BOR marker and join to work in the round.

Ribbing Round: K1, (p2, k2) rep to 3 sts before m, p2, k1.

Rep Ribbing Round until your work measures 1.25 (1.5, 2, 2, 2, 2) inches / [3 (4, 5, 5, 5, 5) cm] from the CO edge.

Thumb Gusset

Change to LARGER needles.

Chevron Set-Up Round: [K10 (11, 14, 15, 16, 17), pm] 3 times, k10 (11, 14, 15, 16, 17).

Round 1: K1, k2tog, k to 1 st before m, m1R, k1, sm, k1, m1L, k to 3 sts before m, ssk, k1, sm, k1, k2tog, k to 1 st before m, m1R, k1, sm, k1, m1L, k to 3 sts before m, ssk, k1.

Round 2: K all, sm as you come to them.

Rep Rounds 1 and 2 an additional 2 (2, 3, 3, 3, 4) times.

In the following round, you will increase one st and place a single st marker. This st is the base of the thumb gusset, and the additional marker will be at the outer edge of the thumb gusset.

Round 3 (Thumb Gusset set-up): M1L, pm, k1, k2tog, k to 1 st before m, m1R, k1, sm, k1, m1L, k to 3 sts before m, ssk, k1, sm, k1, k2tog, k to 1 st before m, m1R, k1, sm, k1, m1L, k to 3 sts before m, ssk, k1. [1 st inc; 41 (45, 57, 61, 65, 69) sts]

Round 4: M1R, k1, m1L, sm, (k to m, sm) 3 times, k to end. [2 sts inc; 43 (47, 59, 63, 67, 71) sts]

Round 5: K3, sm, k1, k2tog, k to 1 st before m, m1R, k1, sm, k1, m1L, k to 3 sts before m, ssk, k1, sm, k1, k2tog, k to 1 st before m, m1R, k1, sm, k1, m1L, k to 3 sts before m, ssk, k1.

Round 6: M1R, k to m, m1L, sm, (k to m, sm) 3 times, k to end. [2 sts inc; 45 (49, 61, 65, 69, 73) sts]

Round 7: K to m, sm, k1, k2tog, k to 1 st before m, m1R, k1, sm, k1, m1L, k to 3 sts before m, ssk, k1, sm, k1, k2tog, k to 1 st before m, m1R, k1, sm, k1, m1L, k to 3 sts before m, ssk, k1.

Rep Rounds 6 and 7 an additional 4 (5, 7, 8, 8, 8) times until you have 53 (59, 75, 81, 85, 89) sts on your needles.

Round 8: K all.

Round 9: K to m, sm, k1, k2tog, k to 1 st before m, m1R, k1, sm, k1, m1L, k to 3 sts before m, ssk, k1, sm, k1, k2tog, k to 1 st before m, m1R, k1, sm, k1, m1L, k to 3 sts before m, ssk, k1.

Rep Rounds 8 and 9 once more.

Thumb

Place held sts on your LARGER DPNs. Knit across all held sts. Pick up and knit 5 sts from the gap where the thumb and mitten do not meet. Place a BOR marker and join to work in the round. You should now have 18 (20, 24, 26, 26, 26) sts on your needles.

Next Round: K13 (15, 19, 21, 21, 21), ssk, k1, k2tog. [2 sts dec; 16 (18, 22, 24, 24, 24) sts total]

Work in stockinette stitch (k every round) until thumb measures 1 (1.5, 2, 2.25, 2.25, 2.5) inches [2.5 (4, 5, 6, 6, 6.5) cm] or 0.25 inches (0.6 cm) less than desired length.

Decrease Round 1: Ssk to end. [8 (9, 11, 12, 12, 12) sts dec; 8 (9, 11, 12, 12, 12) sts total]

Child, Adult S: Ssk - (4, 5, -, -, -) times, k1. [- (4, 5, -, -, -) sts dec; - (4, 6, -, -, -) sts total]

Toddler, Adult M, L, XL: Ssk to end. [4 (-, -, 6, 6, 6) sts dec; 4 (-, -, 6, 6, 6) sts total]

Break yarn, leaving a 6-inch (15-cm) tail. Using a tapestry needle, pull the yarn through 4 (4, 6, 6, 6, 6) remaining live sts and pull the hole closed.

Next Round: Sl13 (15, 19, 21, 21, 21) sts purlwise onto a piece of scrap yarn to hold for the thumb, k to end.

You should now have 40 (44, 56, 60, 64, 68) on your needles for the Palm and 13 (15, 19, 21, 21, 21) sts on hold for the Thumb.

Palm

Round 1: K1, k2tog, k to 1 st before m, m1R, k1, sm, k1, m1L, k to 3 sts before m, ssk, k1, sm, k1, k2tog, k to 1 st before m, m1R, k1, sm, k1, m1L, k to 3 sts before m, ssk, k1.

Round 2: K all.

Rep Rounds 1 and 2 until the Palm measures 2.75 (4, 4.75, 5, 5.25, 5.5) inches [7 (10, 12, 13, 13.5, 14) cm] from the top of the thumb gusset, or your desired length.

Break yarn, leaving a 24-inch (61-cm) tail. Place the first 20 (22, 28, 30, 32, 34) sts onto one DPN. Place the second 20 (22, 28, 30, 32, 34) sts onto another DPN. Use the Kitchener Stitch (see page 181) to graft the stitches of the first needle together with the sts of the second needle.

Finishing

Weave in all ends. For the best results, be sure to wet block your finished mittens. Soak the mittens in cold water, squeezing to remove air bubbles. Squeeze out the water, but do not wring. Roll the mittens in a dry towel, burrito-style, and press on it to remove excess water. Lay flat to dry, using a measuring tape to be sure they are laid out with the correct dimensions. The increases and decreases in this mitten create a rather pointy top at the tip of the palm. For a better fitting mitten, I recommend giving the top of your mitten a more rounded end with careful blocking. To do this, you can use a mitten blocker, blocking pins or gentle stretching along the top edge while the mitten is quite damp.

Sharp Curve Mittens
Skill Level: Advanced

Sometimes when I see a skein of yarn dyed in rainbow colors, I see actual rainbows. When I pulled this beautiful skein of yarn from my knitting bag, I knew that whatever I made with it needed the sharp curve of a real rainbow in the sky. These mittens are a knitting adventure. Knit flat from the center out, this pattern is not like any mitten you have knit before. After binding off around the outer edge of the palms, you will work a short row thumb gusset that will dazzle in self-striping yarn. Although both mittens are worked identically, you can add personality to each mitten by changing the color order.

Construction

Using the Magic Loop method and beginning with the Turkish cast on (see page 179), the front palm of this mitten is knit flat from the center out. The front palm is then set aside, and the back palm is worked identically to the front palm. The front and back palm are joined along the outer edge by using a three-needle bind off (see page 180). Next, the thumb gusset is worked flat using the German Short Rows method (see page 184). After completing the thumb gusset, the thumb is then joined and worked in the round. Finally, the cuff is picked up along the bottom edge of the palm and work in the round.

Maximum Stitches Used for a Self-Striping Row: 130

Sizes

Adult M

See the Finished Measurements on page 22.

NOTE: This pattern was designed to fit an average adult hand. These mittens can comfortably fit with a range of ease from 1 inch (2.5 cm) of negative ease to 0.5 inches (1.25 cm) of positive ease. To check size, determine the circumference of your hand, excluding the thumb, by wrapping a flexible tape measure around the knuckles of your hand. If you would like to adjust the size of your mittens, you can do so by adjusting your gauge or working additional/fewer rows in the Front Palm and Back Palm sections. Any adjustments to your gauge will change your final yardage.

Yarn

- Fingering weight yarn, White Birch Fiber Arts
- (80% superwash merino and 20% nylon, 400 yards / 3.5 ounces [365 m / 100g])
- Sample shown in "Rainbow Warrior"
- 1 skein
- 205 yards (187 m)

Yarn Notes

I knit these mittens using a yarn with two thick stripes: a gray stripe and a rainbow stripe. The rainbow stripe contains multiple mini-stripes that are a pleasure to knit in each of the different sections of this mitten. They were especially exciting when working the short rows in the thumb gusset!

Needles

Two sets of US 1 (2.25 mm) 60-inch (150-cm) circular needles for Magic Loop, or as required to meet gauge

DPNs or needles for small circumference knitting in the same size

Gauge

28 stitches and 40 rows = 4 inches (10 cm) in stockinette stitch after blocking

Notions

- Tape measure
- 2 stitch markers
- Scissors
- Tapestry needle

Finished Measurements

A. **Palm Circumference:** 7.5 inches (19 cm)

B. **Palm Length:** 8 inches (20 cm)

C. **Cuff Length:** 1.5 inches (4 cm)

D. **Total Length:** 9.5 inches (24 cm)

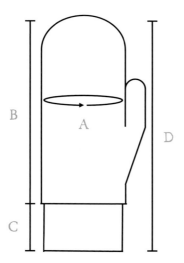

Abbreviations	
BO	bind off
BOR	beginning of round
cdd	central double decrease
CO	cast on
dec	decrease
DPNs	double pointed needles
DS	double stitch
inc	increase
k	knit
k2tog	knit two together
LH	left-hand
m	marker
m1L	make one left
m1R	make one right
p	purl
pm	place marker
rep	repeat
RH	right-hand
sm	slip marker
ssk	slip, slip, knit
st(s)	stitch(es)
WS	wrong side

Pattern

Both mittens are knit identically.

You will begin this pattern using the Turkish cast on method. If this technique is new to you, see page 179 for more info. Typically the Turkish cast on method is used for working knitting projects in the round. For these mittens, you will use this CO to work the palm of the mitten flat from the center out. The design is written to be worked using the Magic Loop technique, in which you use a set of circular knitting needles with a long cord.

Front Palm

Using the Turkish cast on method and your circular needles, CO 104 sts. You should now have 52 sts on each needle.

Set up Row (RS): K all.

You will now turn your work so that the WS of the work is facing you. In the following row, you will be placing 2 st markers. The placement of these st markers indicates where you will be increasing on RS rows to create the semicircle for the fingertips. At the opposite end of your work, you will be creating a flat edge where you will later pick up sts for the wrist ribbing. See Fig. 1 below for an illustration of the palm construction.

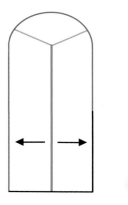

1

Bind Off shown in RED
Cast On shown in BLUE
Arrows indicate directions of knitting

Set up Row (WS): P50, pm, p4, pm, p50.

Row 1 (RS): K to 1 st before m, m1R, k1, sm, m1L, k1, m1L, k2, m1R, k1, m1R, sm, k1, m1L, k to end. [6 sts inc; 110 sts total]

Note: You may find it helpful to place a removable stitch marker in the first stitch of the RS row. This will help you keep track of the beginning of the row so that you do not knit past it and accidentally work in the round.

Row 2 (WS): P all.

Row 3 (RS): K to 1 st before m, m1R, k1, sm, k to m, sm, k1, m1L, k to end. [2 sts inc; 112 sts total]

Row 4 (WS): P all.

Row 5 (RS): K to 1 st before m, m1R, k1, sm, m1L, k to m, m1R, sm, k1, m1L, k to end. [4 sts inc; 116 sts total]

Row 6 (WS): P all.

Rep Rows 3–6 an additional two times. You should have 128 sts on your needles. Work Rows 3 and 4 once more. You should have 130 sts on your needles. You should have 58 sts before the first stitch marker, 14 sts between the two markers and 58 sts after the second stitch marker.

Note: Your palm should measure approximately 3.75 inches (9.5 cm) wide. If you would like to make the circumference of your palm larger, or if you have not yet reached the target width, work in stockinette stitch (k the RS rows, p the WS rows) until you reach your target width. End after completing a WS row. Keep in mind that the width of your palm will equal half of your mitten circumference. Therefore, if you want the circumference of your mitten to be 8 inches (20 cm), then your palm should have a width of 4 inches (10 cm). Make a note of any changes you make to the Front Palm. You will need to make the same changes to the Back Palm.

Break yarn, leaving a 6-inch (15-cm) tail. Set aside the Front Palm while you work the Back Palm.

Back Palm

Using your second set of circular needles, work the Front Palm section once more, but do not break your yarn when you complete the Back Palm.

> Note: If you made modifications to the size of your Front Palm, make the same modifications to the Back Palm. The Front Palms and Back Palms should be identical.

Joining

Align the Front Palm and Back Palm sections so that the WS are together and RS are facing out. Use the three-needle bind off to BO 105 sts. Remove markers as you come to them. This will leave one stitch on your RH needle and 25 live sts on each of the Front Palm and the Back Palm needles. You will have 50 live sts total. Break yarn, leaving a 6-inch (15-cm) tail. Pull the tail through the one stitch left on your RH needle.

> Note: When you work your second mitten, I recommend working the three-needle bind off purlwise. This will make the seam appear identical on both of your mittens when you are wearing them.

Thumb Gusset

In this section, you will create a short row thumb gusset. In order to create the thumb gusset for this mitten, you will be working back and forth from the bottom up. Each short row will attach a stitch from the Front or Back Palm to the Thumb Gusset until you reach Row 19. After Row 19, the short rows will add length to the Thumb Gusset.

Needle Placement: Using your DPNs and beginning at the seam, place 19 sts on your first DPN from the Front Palm. Place 6 sts from the Front Palm and 6 sts from the Back Palm on the second DPN. Place the last 19 sts on your third DPN. See Photo 2.

> Note: If you prefer not to work this section using DPNs, I recommend using a set of 9-inch (23-cm) circular needles. If you are working on circular needles, beginning at the seam, slip the first 19 sts purlwise before starting the Set-Up Row.

In the first row, you will be casting on a single st. I recommend using the Backwards Loop cast on method (see page 177). This st will be CO between the bottom edge of the Front Palm and the Back Palm.

You will begin the Set-Up Row at the beginning of the second needle.

Set-Up Row (RS): K6, CO 1, k6, turn work. [1 st inc; 51 sts total]

Photo 3 shows the mitten after working the Set-Up Row (RS).

Next Row (WS): DS, p13, turn work.

Row 1 (RS): DS, k3, ssk, cdd, k2tog, k4, turn work. [4 sts dec; 47 sts total]

Row 2 (WS): DS, p12, turn work.

Row 3 (RS): DS, k3, ssk, cdd, k2tog, k4, turn work. [4 sts dec; 43 sts total]

Row 4 (WS): DS, p12, turn work.

Row 5 (RS): DS, k3, ssk, cdd, k2tog, k4, turn work. [4 sts dec; 39 sts total]

Row 6 (WS): DS, p12, turn work.

Row 7 (RS): DS, k5, cdd, k6, turn work. [2 sts dec; 37 sts total]

Row 8 (WS): DS, p14, turn work.

Row 9 (RS): DS, k6, cdd, k7, turn work. [2 sts dec; 35 sts total]

Row 10 (WS): DS, p16, turn work.

Row 11 (RS): DS, k7, cdd, k8, turn work. [2 sts dec; 33 sts]

Row 12 (WS): DS, p18, turn work.

Row 13 (RS): DS, k8, cdd, k9, turn work. [2 sts dec; 31 sts]

Row 14 (WS): DS, p20, turn work.

Row 15 (RS): DS, k9, cdd, k10, turn work. [2 sts dec; 29 sts total]

Row 16 (WS): DS, p22, turn work.

Row 17 (RS): DS, k10, cdd, k11, turn work. [2 sts dec; 27 sts total]

Row 18 (WS): DS, p23, turn work.

Row 19 (RS): DS, k10, cdd, k11, turn work. [2 sts dec; 25 sts total]

Row 20 (WS): DS, p14, turn work.

Row 21 (RS): DS, k1, cdd, k2, turn work. [2 sts dec; 23 sts total]

Row 22 (WS): DS, p6, turn work.

Row 23 (RS): DS, k2, cdd, k3, turn work. [2 sts dec; 21 sts total]

Row 24 (WS): DS, p8, turn work.

Row 25 (RS): DS, k10, turn work.

Row 26 (WS): DS, p12, turn work.

Row 27 (RS): DS, k14, turn work.

Row 28 (WS): DS, p15, turn work.

Row 29 (RS): DS, k16, turn work.

Row 30 (WS): DS, p18, turn work.

Row 31 (RS): DS, k20.

Thumb

Using DPNs, pick up and knit 3 sts from the gap where the thumb and mitt do not meet. Place a BOR marker and join to work in the round. You should now have 24 sts on your needles. In the first round, the first st is a DS; resolve this DS. Work in stockinette stitch (k every round) until the thumb measures 2.25 inches (5.5 cm) or 0.25 inches (0.6 cm) less than the desired length.

Decrease Round 1: Ssk 12 times. [12 sts dec; 12 sts total]

Decrease Round 2: Ssk 6 times. [6 sts dec; 6 sts total]

Break yarn, leaving a 6-inch (15-cm) tail. Using a tapestry needle, pull yarn through 6 remaining live sts and pull the hole closed.

Cuff

Using DPNs, pick up and knit 46 sts around the circumference of the wrist. Place a BOR marker and join to work in the round. Work 1x1 ribbing (k1, p1) until ribbing measures 1.5 inches (4 cm). BO all sts in pattern. Break yarn, leaving a 6-inch (15-cm) tail.

Finishing

Weave in all ends. For the best results, be sure to wet block your finished mittens. Soak the mittens in cold water, squeezing to remove air bubbles. Squeeze out the water but do not wring. Roll the mittens in a dry towel, burrito-style, and press on it to remove excess water. Lay flat to dry, using a measuring tape to be sure they are laid out with the correct dimensions. You can use blocking pins to pin the arch at the top of the mitten. This will help the curve of the mitten lay flat after it has dried.

Rainbow Adventure Fingerless Mitts

Skill Level: Adventurous Beginner

These fingerless mitts are a fuss-free project that will fly off your knitting needles. Using a combination of ribbing and twisted ribbing, you never have to work a single complicated stitch. The ribbing allows these mitts to stretch and adapt to the shape of your hands, making this a great project for gift knitting. The long cuff means that there will never be a gap between your mitt and your coat sleeve. Knit in self-striping yarn, these mitts go from easy and practical to downright exhilarating. This pattern includes a helpful tip for transitioning between your stripes as you work in ribbing and twisted ribbing. This little skill will make your stripes look tidy and professional and come in handy later when you knit hats or sleeves. Let your yarn take you on a rainbow adventure while you knit these sweet little fingerless mitts.

Construction

Each fingerless mitt is knit seamlessly in the round from the bottom up. The thumb gusset is created using a nontraditional method of adding stitches to the palm using simple increases. After working the thumb gusset, the thumb stitches are then placed on hold while the palm is completed. Finally, the stitches for the thumb cuff are placed back on the needles and joined and worked in the round.

Maximum Stitches Used for a Self-Striping Round: 40 (44, 52, 56, 60, 68)

Sizes

Toddler (Child, Adult S, Adult M, Adult L, Adult XL)

See the Finished Measurements on page 30 to choose your size.

NOTE: To find your size, determine the circumference of your hand, excluding the thumb, by wrapping a flexible tape measure around the knuckles of your hand. Choose a size approximately 1 inch (2.5 cm) smaller than the circumference of your hand. These mitts are intended to fit snugly. If in doubt, go down a size.

Yarn

- Worsted weight yarn, Must Stash Sweater Weather
- (100% merino, 220 yards / 3.5 ounces [183 m / 100 g])
- Sample shown in "Vespa"
- 1 skein
- 65 (85, 100, 105, 110, 120) yards / [60 (78, 92, 96, 101, 110) m]

Yarn Notes

I chose a plied worsted yarn for these fingerless mitts. I like to wear my fingerless mitts on top of thinner gloves and mittens for extra warmth and an extra pop of color. The plied worsted merino gives my mitts additional durability.

Needles

US 4 (3.5 mm) DPNs, or as required to meet gauge

Gauge

24 stitches and 30 rounds = 4 inches (10 cm) in 3x1 ribbing, unstretched, in the round, after blocking

Notions

- Tape measure
- 2 stitch markers
- Scissors
- Scrap yarn
- Tapestry needle

Finished Measurements

Sample shown is Adult M.

A. **Palm Circumference:** 4.75 (5.25, 6, 6.75, 7.25, 8) inches / [12 (13.5, 15.5, 17, 18.5, 20.5) cm]

B. **Total Length:** 4.75 (5.5, 7, 7.5, 7.5, 8.5) inches / [12 (14, 17, 19, 19, 21.5) cm]

Abbreviations	
BOR	beginning of round
CO	cast on
DPNs	double pointed needles
inc	increase
k	knit
m	marker
m1L	make one left
m1R	make one right
p	purl
pm	place marker
rep	repeat
rm	remove marker
sl	slip
sm	slip marker
st(s)	stitch(es)
tbl	through the back loop

Pattern

These mitts are not knit identically. You will find separate instructions for working the right and left mitts.

Note: When using a self-striping yarn, on the first round of each new color, knit all the purl sts in that round. You will still work all increases and "k1 tbl" as per the instructions. However, substituting a knit st for a purl st in the color change rounds will give you a clean color transition. When you have completed the first round of the new color, continue to work the purl sts according to the pattern.

Right Mitt

CO 28 (32, 36, 40, 44, 48) sts. Place a BOR marker and join to work in the round.

Set-Up Round: (P1, k3) 4 (5, 5, 6, 7, 7) times, pm, (p1, k1 tbl) 6 (6, 8, 8, 8, 10) times.

Cuff Ribbing Round: (P1, k3) rep to m, sm, (p1, k1 tbl) rep to end.

Rep the Cuff Ribbing Round until your work measures 1.75 (2.25, 2.5, 3, 3, 3.25) inches [4.5 (6, 6.5, 7.5, 7.5, 8.5) cm] from the CO edge.

> Note: This fingerless mitt has a nontraditional thumb gusset. You may need to work several rounds for the construction of the mitten to become clear.

Thumb Gusset Round 1: M1L, (p1, k3) rep to m, sm, (p1, k1 tbl) rep to end. [1 st inc]

Thumb Gusset Round 2: M1L, k1, (p1, k3) rep to m, sm, (p1, k1 tbl) rep to end. [1 st inc]

Thumb Gusset Round 3: M1L, k2, (p1, k3) rep to m, sm, (p1, k1 tbl) rep to end. [1 st inc]

Thumb Gusset Round 4: M1L, k3, (p1, k3) rep to m, sm, (p1, k1 tbl) rep to end. [1 st inc]

Rep Thumb Gusset Rounds 1–4 an additional 2 (2, 3, 3, 3, 4) times. You should have 40 (44, 52, 56, 60, 68) sts on your needles.

Palm Set-Up Round: (P1, k3) rep to m, rm, sl12 (12, 16, 16, 16, 20) sts onto a piece of scrap yarn to hold for the thumb.

You should now have 28 (32, 36, 40, 44, 48) sts on your needles. With the BOR marker in place, rejoin to work in the round.

Palm Ribbing Round: (P1, k3) rep to end.

Rep the Palm Ribbing Round until your palm ribbing measures approximately 0.75 (1, 1.25, 1.5, 1.5, 1.75) inches [2 (2.5, 3, 4, 4, 4.5) cm] from the top of the thumb gusset or 0.5 (0.5, 0.75, 0.75, 0.75, 0.75) inches [1.25 (1.25, 2, 2, 2, 2) cm] less than your desired length.

Upper Cuff Ribbing Round: (P1, k1 tbl) rep to end.

Work the Upper Cuff Ribbing Round an additional 3 (3, 5, 5, 5, 5) times or until you reach your desired length. BO all sts in pattern. Break yarn, leaving a 6-inch (15-cm) tail.

Thumb Set-Up: Place held thumb sts onto your DPNs. (P1, k1 tbl) 6 (6, 8, 8, 8, 10) times. Pick up and knit 2 sts across the gap where the thumb and mitten do not meet. Place a BOR marker and join to work in the round.

You should now have 14 (14, 18, 18, 18, 22) sts on your needles.

Thumb Ribbing Round: (P1, k1 tbl) rep to end.

Rep Thumb Ribbing Round an additional 4 (5, 6, 6, 6, 7) times or until you reach your desired length. BO all sts in pattern. Break yarn, leaving a 6-inch (15-cm) tail.

Left Mitt

CO 28 (32, 36, 40, 44, 48) sts. Place a BOR marker and join to work in the round.

Set-Up Round: (K1 tbl, p1) 6 (6, 8, 8, 8, 10) times, pm, (k3, p1) 4 (5, 5, 6, 7, 7) times.

Cuff Ribbing Round: (K1 tbl, p1) rep to m, sm, (k3, p1) rep to end.

Rep the Cuff Ribbing Round until your work measures 1.75 (2.25, 2.5, 3, 3, 3.25) inches [4.5 (6, 6.5, 7.5, 7.5, 8.5) cm] from the CO edge.

Thumb Gusset Round 1: (K1 tbl, p1) rep to m, sm, (k3, p1) rep to end, m1R. [1 st inc]

Thumb Gusset Round 2: (K1 tbl, p1) rep to m, sm, (k3, p1) rep to last st, k1, m1R. [1 st inc]

Thumb Gusset Round 3: (K1 tbl, p1) rep to m, sm, (k3, p1) rep to last 2 sts, k2, m1R. [1 st inc]

Thumb Gusset Round 4: (K1 tbl, p1) rep to m, sm, (k3, p1) rep to last 3 sts, k3, m1R. [1 st inc]

Rep Thumb Gusset Rounds 1–4 an additional 2 (2, 3, 3, 3, 4) times. You should have 40 (44, 52, 56, 60, 68) sts on your needles.

Palm Set-Up Round: Sl12 (12, 16, 16, 16, 20) sts onto a piece of scrap yarn to hold for the thumb, rm, (k3, p1) rep to end.

You should now have 28 (32, 36, 40, 44, 48) sts on your needles. With the BOR marker in place, rejoin to work in the round.

Palm Ribbing Round: (K3, p1) rep to end.

Rep the Palm Ribbing Round until your palm ribbing measures approximately 0.75 (1, 1.25, 1.5, 1.5, 1.75) inches [2 (2.5, 3, 4, 4, 4.5) cm] from the top of the thumb gusset or 0.5 (0.5, 0.75, 0.75, 0.75, 0.75) inches [1.25 (1.25, 2, 2, 2, 2) cm] less than your desired length.

Upper Cuff Ribbing Round: (K1 tbl, p1) rep to end.

Work the Upper Cuff Ribbing Round an additional 3 (3, 5, 5, 5, 5) times, or until you reach your desired length. BO all sts in pattern. Break yarn, leaving a 6-inch (15-cm) tail.

Thumb Set-Up: Place held thumb sts onto your DPNs. (K1 tbl, p1) 6 (6, 8, 8, 8, 10) times. Pick up and knit 2 sts across the gap where the thumb and mitten do not meet. Place a BOR marker and join to work in the round.

You should now have 14 (14, 18, 18, 18, 22) sts on your needles.

Thumb Ribbing Round: (K1 tbl, p1) rep to end.

Rep Thumb Ribbing Round an additional 4 (5, 6, 6, 6, 7) times, or until you reach your desired length. BO all sts in pattern. Break yarn, leaving a 6-inch (15-cm) tail.

Finishing

Weave in all ends. For the best results, be sure to wet block your finished mitts. Soak the mitts in cold water, squeezing to remove air bubbles. Squeeze out the water but do not wring. Roll the mitts in a dry towel, burrito-style, and press on it to remove excess water. Lay flat to dry, using a measuring tape to be sure they are laid out with the correct dimensions.

Leapfrog Mittens

Skill Level: Intermediate

The only thing that can possibly make a skein of self-striping yarn more fun is a coordinating mini skein. I knit these mittens using a "toes and heels" sock set. Since socks are such a popular project for self-striping yarn, dyers often create beautiful little yarn kits that include a solid yarn and a perfectly paired self-striping yarn. The great thing about having a coordinating mini skein for this pattern is that you don't have to think about what color makes the most sense with your beautiful self-striping yarn—the dyer does it for you. The Leapfrog Mittens use these "toes and heels" sets in a new way. These mittens are knit in the round from the bottom up. The beginning of this project is knit like a traditional mitten, but once you reach the palm, the fun begins. Using short rows, the stripes take a leap and hop right over a fun triangular section of solid-colored yarn.

Construction

Each mitten is knit seamlessly in the round from the bottom up. The thumb gusset is created using simple increases. The thumb stitches are then placed on hold while the palm is completed. Two short row wedges are created using the German Short Rows method (see page 184). The top of the mitten is shaped using decreases and then joined with the Kitchener Stitch method (see page 181). Finally, the thumb stitches are placed back on the needles and joined and worked in the round.

Maximum Stitches Used for a Self-Striping Round: 48 (56, 68, 76, 80, 86)

Sizes

Toddler (Child, Adult S, Adult M, Adult L, Adult XL)

See the Finished Measurements on page 34 to choose your size.

NOTE: To find your size, determine the circumference of your hand, excluding the thumb, by wrapping a flexible tape measure around the knuckles of your hand. Choose a size approximately 0.5 inches (1.25 cm) smaller than the circumference of your hand.

Yarn

- Fingering weight yarn, Lollipop Yarn Quintessential

- (80% superwash merino and 20% nylon, 410 yards / 3.5 ounces [375 m / 100 g])

- Sample shown in "Life Is Beautiful" (MC, self-striping) and "Friendship" (CC, brown)

- 1 skein of MC and 1 mini skein of CC

- **Main Color:** 110 (130, 140, 145, 155, 170) yards / [100 (119, 128, 133, 142, 156) m]

- **Contrasting Color:** 15 (20, 25, 30, 35, 40) yards / [14 (18, 23, 28, 32, 37) m]

Yarn Notes

I knit these mittens using a two-ply merino/nylon blend. I love knitting mittens using a yarn with nylon in it. The nylon in this yarn makes the mittens especially durable without sacrificing softness.

Needles

US 2 (2.75 mm) and US 1 (2.25 mm) DPNs or needles for small circumference knitting, or as required to meet gauge

Gauge

32 stitches and 40 rows = 4 inches (10 cm) in stockinette stitch on LARGER needles in the round after blocking

Notions

Tape measure

2 stitch markers

Scissors

Scrap yarn

Tapestry needle

Finished Measurements

Sample shown is Adult S.

A. **Palm Circumference:** 4.5 (5, 6, 7, 7.5, 8) inches / [11.5 (12.5, 15, 17.5, 19, 20.5) cm]

B. **Palm Length:** 5 (6.5, 7.75, 8.25, 8.5, 9) inches / [12.5 (16.5, 19.5, 21, 21.5, 23) cm]

C. **Cuff Length:** 1.25 (1.5, 2, 2, 2, 2) inches / [3 (3.5, 5, 5, 5, 5) cm]

D. **Total Length:** 6.25 (8, 9.75, 10.25, 10.5, 11) inches / [16 (20.5, 25, 26, 26.5, 28) cm]

Abbreviations	
BOR	beginning of round
CC	contrast color
CO	cast on
dec	decrease
DS	double stitch
inc	increase
k	knit
k2tog	knit two together
m	marker
MC	main color
m1L	make one left
m1R	make one right
p	purl
pm	place marker
rep	repeat
RS	right side
sl	slip
sm	slip marker
ssk	slip, slip, knit
st(s)	stitch(es)
WS	wrong side

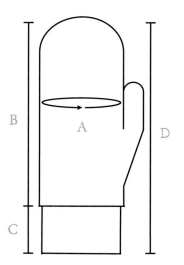

Pattern

Both mittens are knit identically.

Cuff

Using SMALLER needles and MC, CO 36 (40, 48, 56, 60, 64) sts. Place a BOR marker and join to work in the round. Work 2x2 ribbing (k2, p2) until your work measures 1.25 (1.5, 2, 2, 2, 2) inches [3 (3.5, 5, 5, 5, 5) cm] from the CO edge. If you would like to add length to your mittens, do so here by working additional ribbing. Remember that adding additional rounds will increase your final yardage.

Change to LARGER needles and knit 3 (4, 5, 6, 6, 6) rounds.

Thumb Gusset

Set-Up Round: K1, pm, k to end.

Round 1: M1R, k1, m1L, sm, k to end. [2 sts inc; 38 (42, 50, 58, 62, 66) sts total]

Round 2: K all.

Round 3: M1R, k to m, m1L, sm, k to end. [2 sts inc; 40 (44, 52, 60, 64, 68) sts total]

Round 4: K all.

Rep Rounds 3 and 4 an additional 4 (6, 8, 8, 8, 9) times until you have 48 (56, 68, 76, 80, 86) sts on your needles.

Knit 2 (3, 3, 4, 4, 4) rounds.

Next Round: Sl13 (17, 21, 21, 21, 23) sts purlwise onto a piece of scrap yarn to hold for the thumb, CO 1 st using the Backwards Loop cast on, rejoin to work in the round, k to end.

You should now have 36 (40, 48, 56, 60, 64) sts on your needles for the Palm and 13 (17, 21, 21, 21, 23) sts on hold for the Thumb.

Palm

Knit 2 (3, 4, 5, 5, 5) rounds.

You will now begin working short rows.

In this section, you will be working short rows to build up the outer edge of the mitten. Each time you work repeats of Rows 3 and 4, you will be leaving one st between each DS.

Row 1 (RS): K to last st, turn work.

Row 2 (WS): DS, p to last st, turn work.

Row 3 (RS): DS, k to 1 st before last DS, turn work.

Row 4 (WS): DS, p to 1 st before last DS, turn work.

Rep Rows 3 and 4 an additional 6 (7, 9, 11, 12, 13) times. You should have 6 sts between the last 2 DS sts.

Next Row (RS): DS, k4.

You should have 4 sts between the last 2 DS sts. You will not be at the beginning of the round. Instead, you will be just past the center of the round. Do not break MC.

Slip all sts and DS sts purlwise (without resolving or changing the DS sts in any way) until you reach the BOR marker.

Join CC.

You will no longer be working short rows. You will instead be working in the round.

K one round, resolving all DS sts as you come to them.

P one round.

K one round.

You are now ready to begin working a second short row wedge. In this section, you will be working short rows to build up the inner edge of the mitten.

Row 5 (RS): K2, turn work.

Row 6 (WS): DS, p1, sl BOR m, p2, turn work.

Row 7 (RS): DS, k to BOR m, sm, k to last DS, resolve DS, k2, turn work.

Row 8 (WS): DS, p to BOR m, sm, p to last DS, resolve DS, p2, turn work.

Rep Rows 7 and 8 an additional 6 (7, 9, 11, 12, 13) times. You should have 4 sts between the last two DS sts.

Next Row (RS): DS, k to BOR m.

You will no longer be working short rows. You will be working in the round.

K one round, resolving all DS sts as you come to them.

P one round.

Break CC, leaving a 6-inch (15-cm) tail.

Remove the BOR marker. Sl18 (20, 24, 28, 30, 32) sts purlwise, place the BOR marker. This is the new beginning of the round.

Join the MC.

Knit every round until your work measures 2.25 (3, 3.25, 3.5, 3.75, 4) inches [6 (7.5, 8, 9, 9.5, 10) cm] from the top of the thumb gusset OR until the palm measures 1 (1, 1.5, 1.5, 1.5, 1.5) inches [2.5 (2.5, 3.5, 4, 4, 4) cm] less than your desired length.

Top Shaping

Round 1: K1, ssk, k12 (14, 18, 22, 24, 26), k2tog, k1, pm, k1, ssk, k12 (14, 18, 22, 24, 26), k2tog, k1. [4 sts dec; 32 (34, 44, 52, 56, 60) sts total]

Round 2: K all.

Round 3: (K1, ssk, k to 3 sts before m, k2tog, k1, sm) 2 times. [4 sts dec; 28 (32, 40, 48, 52, 56) sts total]

Round 4: K all.

Rep Rounds 3 and 4 until you have 24 (28, 28, 36, 40, 40) sts.

Rep Round 3 ONLY until you have 12 (16, 16, 20, 20, 20) sts.

Break yarn, leaving an 18-inch (46-cm) tail. Place the first 6 (8, 8, 10, 10, 10) sts onto one DPN. Place the second 6 (8, 8, 10, 10, 10) sts onto another DPN. Use the Kitchener Stitch method (see page 181) to graft the stitches of the first needle together with the sts of the second needle.

Thumb

Place held sts on your LARGER DPNs. Using the MC, knit across all held sts. Pick up and knit 3 sts from the gap where the thumb and mitten do not meet. Place a BOR marker and join to work in the round. You should now have 16 (20, 24, 24, 24, 26) sts on your needles. Work in stockinette stitch (k every round) until the thumb measures 1 (1.5, 2, 2.25, 2.25, 2.5) inches [2.5 (4, 5, 5.5, 5.5, 6.5) cm] or 0.25 inches (0.6 cm) less than desired length.

Decrease Round 1: Ssk to end. [8 (10, 12, 12, 12, 13) sts dec; 8 (10, 12, 12, 12, 13) sts total]

Toddler, Child, Adult S, M and L: Ssk to end. [4 (5, 6, 6, 6, -) sts dec; 4 (5, 6, 6, 6, -) sts total]

Adult XL: Ssk 6 times, k1. [- (-, -, -, -, 6) sts dec; - (-, -, -, -, 7) sts total]

Break yarn, leaving a 6-inch (15-cm) tail. Using a tapestry needle, pull the yarn through 4 (5, 6, 6, 6, 7) remaining live sts and pull the hole closed.

Finishing

Weave in all ends. For the best results, be sure to wet block your finished mittens. Soak the mittens in cold water, squeezing to remove air bubbles. Squeeze out the water, but do not wring. Roll the mittens in a dry towel, burrito-style, and press on it to remove excess water. Lay flat to dry, using a measuring tape to be sure they are laid out with the correct dimensions.

Glitz Mittens

Skill Level: Intermediate

The Glitz Mittens are packed with hearts and a sprinkling of speckles. These little speckles add some glamour to your mittens and also create a lovely place for your self-striping yarn to transition smoothly from one color to the next. The Glitz Mittens are knit in the round, from the bottom up, using stranded colorwork. The self-striping yarn creates a big impact in this project with little effort and just a few ends to weave in. If you've been wondering about what your self-striping yarn would look like in a stranded colorwork project, these mittens are a wonderful place to test out your curiosity.

Construction

This mitten is knit seamlessly from the bottom up in the round. The thumb gusset is created using simple increases. The thumb stitches are then placed on hold while the palm is completed. The top of the mitten is shaped using decreases and then joined with the Kitchener Stitch method (page 181). Finally, the thumb stitches are placed back on the needles and joined and worked in the round.

Maximum Stitches Used for a Self-Striping Round: 78

Sizes

Adult M

See the Finished Measurements on page 40.

NOTE: This pattern was designed to fit an average adult hand. These mittens can comfortably fit with a range of ease from 0.5 inches (1.25 cm) of negative ease to 0.5 inches (1.25 cm) of positive ease. To check size, determine the circumference of your hand, excluding the thumb, by wrapping a flexible tape measure around the knuckles of your hand. If you would like to adjust the size of your mittens, you can do so by adjusting your gauge or working additional/fewer rows in the Front Palm and Back Palm sections. Any adjustments to your gauge will change your final yardage.

Yarn

- Fingering weight yarn, Mudpunch Slash Self-Striping Sock
- (80% superwash merino and 20% nylon, 385 yards / 3.8 ounces [352 m / 110 g]), MC
- Sport weight yarn, Lolodidit Guernsey Sport
- (85% merino and 15% mulberry silk, 325 yards / 3.5 ounces [297 m / 100 g]), CC
- Samples shown in "Harmony Rainbow" (MC, self-striping) and "Naked Hippo" (CC, gray)
- 1 skein of MC and 1 skein of CC
- **Main Color:** 155 yards (142 m)
- **Contrasting Color:** 100 yards (91 m)

Yarn Notes

I chose to knit these mittens using a heavy fingering weight yarn for the self-striping and a sport weight yarn for the solid. This made my mittens particularly warm and squishy by creating a dense fabric.

Needles

US 3 (3.25 mm) DPNs or needles for small circumference knitting, or as required to meet gauge

US 2 (2.75 mm) DPNs or needles for small circumference knitting

Gauge

30 stitches and 38 rows = 4 inches (10 cm) in colorwork motif in the round after blocking

Notions

- Tape measure
- 1 stitch marker
- Scissors
- Scrap yarn
- Tapestry needle

Finished Measurements

A. **Palm Circumference:** 7.75 inches (19.5 cm)

B. **Palm Length:** 8 inches (20.5 cm)

C. **Cuff Length:** 1.75 inches (4.5 cm)

D. **Total Length:** 9.75 inches (24.5 cm)

Abbreviations	
BOR	beginning of round
CC	contrast color
CO	cast on
DPNs	double pointed needles
k	knit
m	marker
MC	main color
m1L	make one left
m1R	make one right
p	purl
rep	repeat
sl1p	slip one purlwise
ssk	slip, slip, knit
st(s)	stitch(es)
wyib	with yarn in back

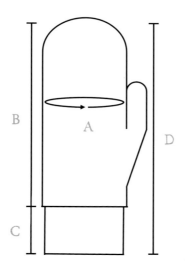

Pattern

Both mittens are knit identically.

Cuff

Using MC and SMALLER needles, CO 56 sts. Place a BOR marker and join to work in the round.

Work 2x2 ribbing (k2, p2) until your cuff measures 1.75 inches (4.5 cm) from CO edge.

Note: When using a self-striping yarn, knit the first round of each new color. When you have completed the first round of the new color, continue working 2x2 ribbing until you reach the target length.

Palm & Thumb Gusset

Change to LARGER needles. Join CC and k one round.

Palm Set-Up Round: Sl1p wyib, k27, m1R, k28, m1L. [2 sts increased; 58 sts total]

Work Palm & Thumb Gusset Chart on pages 42–3.

On Round 7 you will begin working the thumb gusset.

After Round 28, the thumb gusset is complete. On Round 29, work the first 29 sts according to the chart. Place the next 21 thumb sts on scrap yarn to be knit later. CO one st in CC (this st is represented in the Palm & Thumb Gusset Chart in Round 29 as column 40). [58 sts]

Continue to work Palm & Thumb Gusset Chart. When you have completed the chart, break CC, leaving a 12-inch (30.5-cm) tail. Break MC, leaving a 6-inch (15-cm) tail. Divide the front and back sts evenly onto two DPNs. To close the top, use your CC to graft the sts on the front needle to the sts on the back needle using the Kitchener Stitch method (see page 181).

Thumb

Place the 21 held sts for the thumb onto DPNs. Join CC.

Round 1: K all in CC. Pick up and knit 3 sts across the gap. Place a BOR marker and join to work in the round. [24 sts]

Join MC.

Round 2: (K1 CC, k1 MC) rep to end.

Round 3: K all in CC.

Round 4: (K1 MC, k1 CC) rep to end.

Round 5: K all in CC.

Rep Rounds 2–5 until thumb measures 2.5 inches (6.5 cm) or 0.25 inches (0.6 cm) less than your desired length.

Break MC, leaving a 6-inch (15-cm) tail. You will continue working in CC only.

Decrease Round 1: Ssk 12 times. [12 sts dec; 12 sts total]

Decrease Round 2: Ssk 6 times. [6 sts dec; 6 sts total]

Break yarn, leaving a 6-inch (15-cm) tail. Using a tapestry needle, pull yarn through 6 remaining live sts and pull the hole closed.

Finishing

Weave in all ends. For the best results, be sure to wet block your finished mittens. Soak the mittens in cold water, squeezing to remove air bubbles. Squeeze out the water, but do not wring. Roll the mittens in a dry towel, burrito-style, and press on it to remove excess water. Lay flat to dry, using a measuring tape to be sure they are laid out with the correct dimensions.

Chart Instructions

To work charts, begin at the bottom right corner and work right to left.

(Continued)

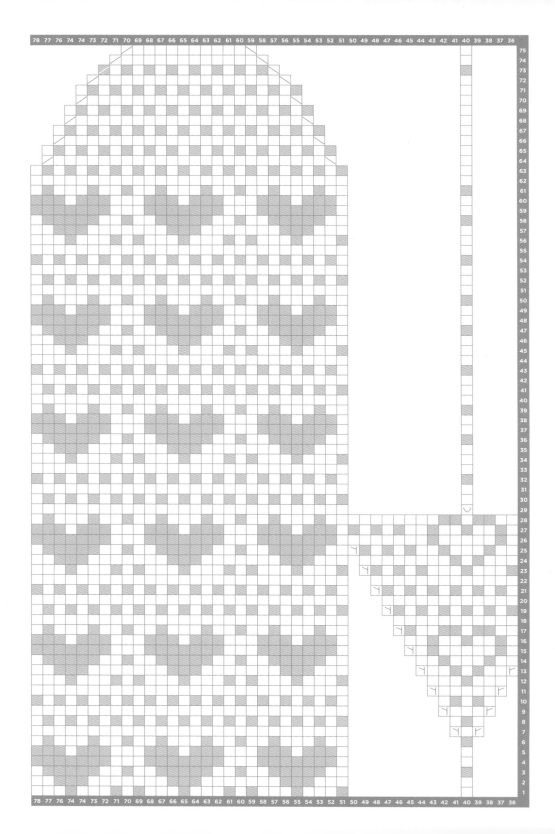

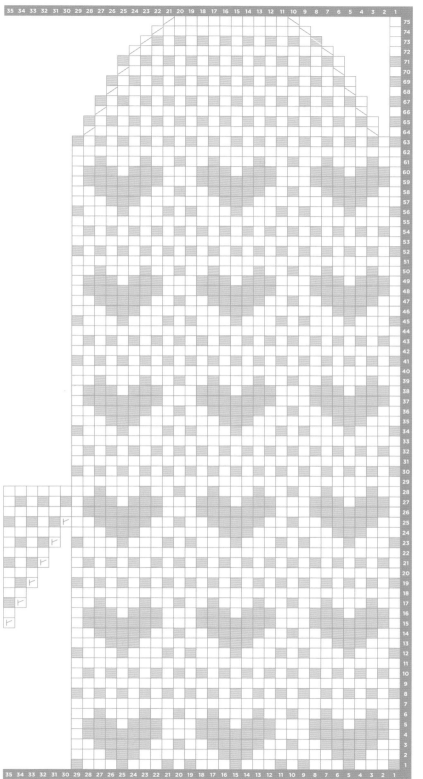

Vibrant Hats

That Knit Up Fast

My husband likes gray. And brown. Oh, and dark green. He doesn't have any flashy shirts or bright jackets. He likes to keep his wardrobe simple and practical, but in the winter, he makes an exception for hats. Okay, nothing crazy—his hat is blue. But still, that blue is a happy blue. Not everyone will wear a neon sweater, but hats are a different story. A hat knit in a bright self-striping yarn is exactly what you want to grab as you walk out the door on a cold, gray day.

The projects in this chapter are the perfect place to get hat-venturous. This chapter is packed with surprising constructions that are terrific for showcasing skeins in vibrant colors. The vertical brim in the Sidelong Glance Hat (page 51) uses a quick chevron stitch that will have you racing to get to the next stripe. Want a project that will have you asking, "What will hat-pen next?" Try the Everyday Magic Bonnet (page 55) with short rows and decreases that send your stripes in all directions. In these pages you will be bending, layering and rocketing through your stripes in ways your needles have never seen before.

Vibrant colors will add a magical boost to these playful knits. Before you know it, dazzling hats will be flying off your needles, ready to make heads happier all winter long.

Rapid Run Hat

Skill Level: Adventurous Beginner

Do you want to know the perfect recipe for an afternoon of knitting joy? Try this: bulky yarn, a simple pattern and self-striping yarn. This hat is exhilaratingly fast and fun to knit. If you are looking for a last-minute gift knit, look no further. The body of the hat features an easy-to-memorize texture that subtly bends your stripes using increases and decreases. This pattern is a great fit for every size and every skill level. The Rapid Run Hat will go on and off your needles so fast that you will be searching for the perfect pom pom before you know it.

Construction
This hat is worked seamlessly in the round from the bottom up.

Maximum Stitches Used for a Self-Striping Round: 56 (64, 72, 80)

Sizes
Baby (Child, Adult M, Adult L)

See the Finished Measurements on page 48 to choose your size.

Yarn
- Bulky weight yarn, Kirby Wirby Bulky
- (100% superwash merino, 106 yards / 3.5 ounces [97 m / 100 g])
- Samples shown in "Tricked Out Treehouse"
- 1 (1, 2, 2) skeins
- 85 (100, 115, 130) yards / [77 (91, 105, 119) m]

Yarn Notes
This pattern was knit using a three-ply bulky yarn. Plied bulky yarn has beautiful stitch definition. For a hat with a fuzzy halo, consider using a single-ply bulky yarn.

Needles
US 10 (6 mm) 16-inch (40-cm) circular needles (length as appropriate for your size), or as required to meet gauge

DPNs or needles for small circumference in the same size

Gauge
14 stitches and 24 rounds = 4 inches (10 cm) in Rapid Run Motif after blocking

Notions
- 8 stitch markers
- Scissors
- Tapestry needle
- Tape measure

Finished Measurements

I recommend knitting this pattern with zero ease. Samples shown in Adult M.

A. **Circumference:** 16 (18.25, 20.5, 23) inches / [40 (46, 51.5, 57.5) cm]

B. **Brim Length:** 1 (1.25, 1.5, 1.5) inches / [2.5 (3, 4, 4) cm]

C. **Body Length:** 4 (5.25, 6.75, 8) inches / [10 (13, 17, 20) cm]

D. **Crown Length:** 1 (1.25, 1.5, 1.75) inches / [2.5 (3, 4, 4.5) cm]

E. **Total Length:** 6 (7.75, 9.75, 11.25) inches / [15 (19.5, 24.5, 28) cm]

Abbreviations	
BOR	beginning of round
CO	cast on
dec	decrease
DPNs	double pointed needles
k	knit
k2tog	knit two together
m	marker
m1R	make one right
p	purl
pm	place marker
rep	repeat
sm	slip marker
st(s)	stitch(es)

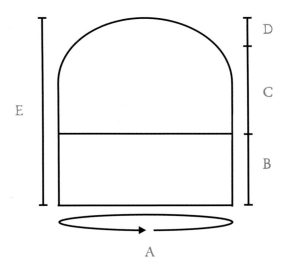

Pattern

Brim

Using circular needles, CO 56 (64, 72, 80) sts. Place a BOR marker and join to work in the round.

Work 1x1 ribbing (k1, p1) until your work measures 1 (1.25, 1.5, 1.5) inches [2.5 (3, 4, 4) cm] from the CO edge.

> **Note:** If you are short on yardage for your self-striping yarn, consider using a solid-colored bulky yarn for the brim of your hat.

Body

K one round.

Round 1: (K5, k2tog, k1, m1R) rep to end.

Round 2: (K4, k2tog, k1, m1R, k1) rep to end.

Round 3: (K3, k2tog, k1, m1R, k2) rep to end.

Round 4: (K2, k2tog, k1, m1R, k3) rep to end.

Round 5: (K1, k2tog, k1, m1R, k4) rep to end.

Round 6: (K2tog, k1, m1R, k5) rep to end.

Round 7: K all.

Round 8: K all.

Work Rounds 1–8 a total of 3 (4, 5, 6) times.

> Note: This hat is knit slightly slouchy. For a fitted hat, work Rounds 1–8 a total of 2 (3, 4, 5) times. You can also make adjustments to the length of your hat by adding knit rounds before working the crown.

Crown

You will now begin working the crown. You will be placing 7 st markers in the Set-Up Round. At the end of the Set-Up Round, you will have 8 st markers, including the BOR marker. After working the Set-Up Round, you will be decreasing every round for the crown. Change to DPNs when you are no longer comfortable working on circular needles.

Set-Up Round: [K7 (8, 9, 10), pm] 7 times, k7 (8, 9, 10).

Decrease Round: (K to 2 sts before m, k2tog, sm) 8 times. [8 sts dec]

Rep Decrease Round until you have 8 sts on your needles.

Break yarn, leaving a 6-inch (15-cm) tail. Using a tapestry needle, pull yarn through 8 remaining live sts.

Finishing

Weave in all ends. For the best results, be sure to wet block your finished hat. Soak the hat in cold water, squeezing to remove air bubbles. Squeeze out the water, but do not wring. Roll the hat in a dry towel, burrito-style, and press on it to remove excess water. Place the hat on a balloon (inflated to approximately your desired head size) to dry. Use a measuring tape to make sure your hat is the correct dimensions.

Sidelong Glance Hat

Skill Level: Intermediate

Have you ever caught someone staring at you out of the corner of their eye? As soon as you look at them, they look away. Maybe they sneak glances at you over and over again. The Sidelong Glance Hat was designed to draw everyone's attention. In this hat, the stripes are worked vertically to create a brim that will have knitters sneaking glances to see just how you knit those pretty chevrons. The vertical stripes in the brim give you the chance to highlight more colors from your striping sequence than you would in a traditional hat. This pattern is great for a yarn with narrow stripes because, even though the brim looks big and dramatic, the rows are short. Not sure you need another hat? Consider skipping the crown and making your new favorite headband.

Construction

This hat is cast on using a Provisional cast on (see page 178). The brim is knit flat from end to end and then joined to create vertical stripes. After the brim is joined in the round, the crown of the hat is picked up along one edge of the brim and worked in the round.

Maximum Stitches Used for a Self-Striping Row: 21 (21, 27, 27)

Sizes

Baby (Child, Adult S/M, Adult L)

See the Finished Measurements on page 52 to choose your size.

Yarn

- Worsted weight yarn, Fibernymph Dye Works Cozy

- (100% superwash merino, 220 yards / 3.5 ounces [201 m / 100 g])

- Sample shown in "Positivity" (MC, self-striping) and "Eggplant" (CC, purple)

- 1 skein of MC, 1 skein of CC

- **Main Color:** 55 (70, 85, 95) yards / [50 (64, 78, 87) m]

- **Contrasting Color:** 30 (50, 65, 75) yards / [28 (46, 59, 69) m]

Yarn Notes

This hat was knit using a lovely worsted weight superwash merino. It has great stitch definition, which looks beautiful in the chevron of the brim. The long color repeats make this hat particularly exciting from every angle.

Needles

US 8 (5 mm) and US 9 (5.5 mm) 16-inch (40-cm) circular needles (length as appropriate for your size), or as required to meet gauge

DPNs or needles for small circumference knitting in the larger size needles

Gauge

24 stitches and 22 rounds = 4 inches (10 cm) in Chevron Motif on SMALLER needles after blocking

20 stitches and 20 rounds = 4 inches (10 cm) in stockinette stitch on LARGER needles after blocking

Notions

- 1 stitch marker
- Scissors
- Scrap yarn
- Tapestry needle
- Tape measure

Finished Measurements

I recommend knitting this pattern with zero ease. Samples shown in Adult S/M.

A. **Circumference:** 16 (18, 21, 23) inches / [40.5 (46, 53.5, 58.5) cm]

B. **Brim Length:** 3.5 (3.5, 4.5, 4.5) inches / [9 (9, 11.5, 11.5) cm]

C. **Crown Length:** 2.25 (3.5, 3.75, 4.75) inches / [6 (9, 10, 12) cm]

D. **Total Length:** 5.75 (7, 8.25, 9.25) inches / [14.5 (18, 21, 23.5) cm]

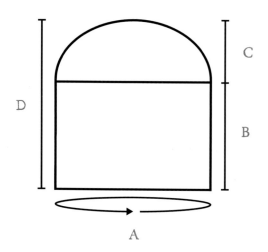

Abbreviations

BOR	beginning of round
CC	contrasting color
CO	cast on
cdd	central double decrease
dec	decrease
DPNs	double pointed needles
k	knit
k2tog	knit two together
m	marker
MC	main color
m1L	make one left
m1R	make one right
p	purl
rep	repeat
RS	right side
sl1p	slip one purlwise
ssk	slip, slip, knit
st(s)	stitch(es)
WS	wrong side
wyib	with yarn in back
wyif	with yarn in front

Pattern

Brim

Begin with a piece of scrap yarn, MC and SMALLER needles. Using a Provisional cast on, CO 21 (21, 27, 27) sts.

Note: If the Provisional cast on method is new to you, see page 178 for more information on how to work this cast on.

Set-Up Row (WS): Sl1p wyif, p to end.

Baby & Child Sizes

Row 1 (RS): K1, ssk, (k1, m1R, k1, m1L, k1, cdd) 2 times, k1, m1R, k1, m1L, k1, k2tog, k1.

Row 2 (WS): Sl1p wyif, p to end.

Adult S/M & Adult L Sizes

Row 1 (RS): K1, ssk, (k2, m1R, k1, m1L, k2, cdd) 2 times, k2, m1R, k1, m1L, k2, k2tog, k1.

Row 2 (WS): Sl1p wyif, p to end.

Rep Rows 1 and 2 according to your size until your work measures approximately 16 (18, 21, 23) inches [40.5 (46, 53.5, 58.5) cm] from the CO edge. End after completing a RS row. If you have achieved row gauge, you will need to work a total of 88 (99, 116, 126) rows. Break yarn, leaving an 18-inch (46-cm) tail for grafting the ends of your brim together.

Note: If you have not achieved row gauge, simply make certain that you work to the target length.

Before joining the ends of your work to create the brim of the hat, I highly recommend placing your sts on a piece of scrap yarn and blocking your work. You will find that blocking your work will change the row and stitch gauge. Once your work is completely dry, if your brim measures longer than your target length, simply remove the additional rows.

Place your live sts back onto your SMALLER needles. Remove the scrap yarn from your Provisional cast on and place these CO sts onto a second set of needles. With a tapestry needle, use the Kitchener Stitch method to graft the two ends together (see page 181). Be careful not to twist your work.

Crown

Using CC and LARGER needles, pick up and knit 48 (60, 72, 84) sts evenly along the upper edge of the brim.

Note: You will not be picking up sts on the slipped st edge of the hat. You will pick up sts on the edge that has no slipped sts. The number of sts picked up for the Crown of the hat will not equal the circumference of the Brim. When picking up sts, you are beginning the process of reducing the size of the hat for the Crown.

Place a BOR marker and join to work in the round.

Next Round: P all.

Next Round: Sl1p wyib, k to end.

Work in stockinette stitch (k every round) until your hat measures 4.25 (5, 6, 6.5) inches [11 (13, 15, 16.5) cm] from the bottom edge of the brim. NOTE: This means you will be measuring the brim and the stockinette together.

Round 1: K3 (4, 5, 6), [cdd, k5 (7, 9, 11)] 5 times, cdd, k2 (3, 4, 5). [12 sts dec; 36 (48, 60, 72) sts]

Round 2: And all EVEN rounds: K all.

Round 3: K2 (3, 4, 5), [cdd, k3 (5, 7, 9)] 5 times, cdd, k1 (2, 3, 4). [12 sts dec; 24 (36, 48, 60) sts]

Round 4: K1 (2, 3, 4), [cdd, k1 (3, 5, 7)] 5 times, cdd, k- (1, 2, 3). [12 sts dec; 12 (24, 36, 48) sts]

Baby ONLY: After working Round 4, skip to Round 8.

Round 5: K- (1, 2, 3), [cdd, k- (1, 3, 5)] 5 times, cdd, k- (-, 1, 2). [12 sts dec; - (12, 24, 36) sts]

Child ONLY: After working Round 5, skip to Round 8.

Round 6: K- (-, 1, 2), [cdd, k- (-, 1, 3)] 5 times, cdd, k- (-, -, 1). [12 sts dec; - (-, 12, 24) sts]

Adult S/M ONLY: After working Round 6, skip to Round 8.

Round 7: K1, (cdd, k1) 5 times, cdd. [12 sts dec; - (-, -, 12) sts]

All Sizes:

Round 8: Cdd 4 times. [8 sts dec; 4 sts]

Break yarn, leaving a 6-inch (15-cm) tail. Using a tapestry needle, pull yarn through 4 remaining live sts.

Finishing

Weave in all ends. For the best results, be sure to wet block your finished hat. Soak the hat in cold water, squeezing to remove air bubbles. Squeeze out the water, but do not wring. Roll the hat in a dry towel, burrito-style, and press on it to remove excess water. Place the hat on a balloon (inflated to approximately your desired head size) to dry. Use a measuring tape to make sure your hat is the correct dimensions.

Everyday Magic Bonnet
Skill Level: Intermediate

I have always loved bonnets. Unlike a traditional hat, bonnets have a sweet, romantic quality that everyone needs in their wardrobe, grown-ups included. Bonnets are a magical playground for self-striping yarn because the rows are short and easy to manage. The Everyday Magic Bonnet is divided into small, seamless sections that create horizontal lines on the sides of your bonnet, a surprising triangle on the back and a striped point to keep your forehead warm. Choose a graphic yarn with clearly defined stripes for this little bonnet, and it won't be long before you have more than just a hat. You will have a dazzling rainbow bonnet that adds magic to your wardrobe every day of the week.

Construction
The Everyday Magic Bonnet is knit seamlessly from the nape of the neck to the front of the forehead. After knitting the left and right side panels, a triangle is picked up and worked on the back of the bonnet. Finally, the top of the bonnet is picked up across the top of the triangle. The side panels are joined using short rows back and decreases. Finally, i-cord ties are picked up and knit at each end of the garter border at the base of the neck.

Maximum Stitches Used for a Self-Striping Row:
48 (52, 58, 64, 70)

Sizes
Baby (Toddler, Child, Adult M, Adult L) intended for head circumference of 16 (17, 19, 21, 23) inches [40 (42.5, 47.5, 52.5, 57.5) cm]

See the Finished Measurements on page 57 to choose your size.

Yarn
- DK weight yarn, Lollipop Yarn Roughage
- (85% superwash merino and 15% nylon tweed, 228 yards / 3.5 ounces [208 m / 100 g])
- Samples shown in "Storm Warnings" (Adult L) and "Nutcase" (Child)
- 1 skein
- 70 (100, 120, 140, 170) yards / [65 (92, 110, 128, 155) m]

Yarn Notes
This pattern was knit using a DK tweed. The tweed yarn gives the stripes an extra dimension of color. YAY! More ways to add color!

Needles
US 5 (3.75 mm) 24-inch (60-cm) circular needles, or as required to meet gauge

2 DPNs in same size for i-cord ties

Gauge

22 stitches and 29 rounds = 4 inches (10 cm) in stockinette stitch after blocking

Notions

- 2 stitch markers
- Scissors
- Tapestry needle
- Scrap yarn
- Tape measure

Finished Measurements

I recommend knitting this pattern with zero ease. Samples shown in Adult L and Child sizes.

A. **Circumference:** 11.5 (12.5, 14.25, 15.5, 18) inches / [29 (32, 36, 39, 45) cm]

B. **Length:** 5.5 (6.5, 8, 9.5, 11) inches / [14 (16.5, 20, 24, 28) cm]

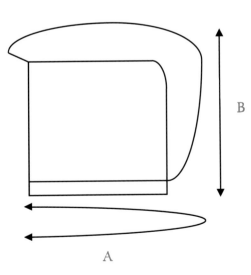

Abbreviations	
BO	bind off
cdd	central double decrease
CO	cast on
dec	decrease
inc	increase
k	knit
k2tog	knit two together
LH	left-hand
m1L	make one left
m1R	make one right
p	purl
pm	place marker
p2tog	purl two together
rep	repeat
RH	right-hand
rm	remove marker
RS	right side
sl	slip
sl1p	slip one purlwise
sm	slip marker
ssk	slip, slip, knit
st(s)	stitch(es)
WS	wrong side
wyib	with yarn in back
wyif	with yarn in front
yo	yarn over

Pattern

Base of the Neck

CO 48 (52, 58, 64, 70) sts.

Knit four rows. End after completing a WS row.

Row 1 (RS): Sl1p wyif, yo, k to end. [1 st inc; 49 (53, 59, 65, 71) sts total]

Row 2 (Division Row) (WS): Sl1p wyif, yo, k1, p22 (24, 27, 30, 33), place the next 25 (27, 30, 33, 36) sts onto a piece of scrap yarn. [1 st inc; 50 (54, 60, 66, 72) sts total]

You should now have 25 (27, 30, 33, 36) sts on your needles. These are your Left Side Panel sts. You should have 25 (27, 30, 33, 36) sts on a piece of scrap yarn. These are your Right Side Panel sts.

Left Side Panel

Row 1 (RS): K to last 2 sts, k2tog. [1 st dec; 24 (26, 29, 32, 35) sts total]

Row 2 (WS): Sl1p wyif, yo, k1, p to end. [1 st inc; 25 (27, 30, 33, 36) sts total]

Rep Rows 1 and 2 until your work measures 4 (4.75, 5.75, 7, 8) inches [10 (12, 14.5, 17.5, 20) cm] from the CO edge. Work Row 1 once more.

> Note: In the following row, you will not work the yarn over after the slipped stitch.

Next Row (WS): Sl1p wyif, k1, p to end.

You should now have 24 (26, 29, 32, 35) sts on your needles. Break yarn, leaving a 6-inch (15-cm) tail.

Place your Left Side Panel sts on a piece of scrap yarn or stitch holder.

Right Side Panel

Place your Right Side Panel sts onto your needles. You should now have 25 (27, 30, 33, 36) sts on your needles. Join yarn and begin on a WS row.

> Note: If you would like your Left Side Panel and Right Side Panel to match, begin this section with the same stripe color that you used at the beginning of the Left Side Panel. Don't stress if your panels do not match exactly, because these panels will be separated by the Center Back Triangle.

Set-Up Row (WS): P to last 3 sts, k1, k2tog. [1 st dec; 24 (26, 29, 32, 35) sts total]

Row 1 (RS): Sl1p wyif, yo, k to end. [1 st inc; 25 (27, 30, 33, 36) sts total]

Row 2 (WS): P to last 3 sts, k1, k2tog. [1 st dec; 24 (26, 29, 32, 35) sts total]

Rep Rows 1 and 2 until your Right Side Panel is the same length as your Left Side Panel. End after completing a WS row. You should now have 24 (26, 29, 32, 35) sts on your needles. Break yarn, leaving a 6-inch (15-cm) tail.

Place your Right Side Panel sts on a piece of scrap yarn or stitch holder. All of your Side Panel sts should now be on scrap yarn or stitch holders.

Center Back Triangle

> Note: Before picking up sts in this section, make sure that your work is not twisted at the base of the neck between the side panels.

With the RS of your work facing you, pick up and knit 13 (15, 19, 23, 27) sts along the inside edge of the Right Side Panel, 1 st between the Side Panels, and 13 (15, 19, 23, 27) sts along the inside edge of the Left Side Panel. See Fig. 1.

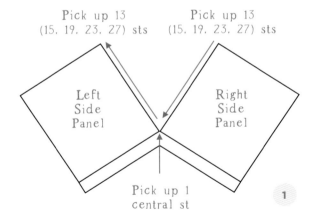

Pick up 13 (15, 19, 23, 27) sts — Pick up 13 (15, 19, 23, 27) sts

Left Side Panel

Right Side Panel

Pick up 1 central st

1

> Note: You will be picking up approximately 1 st for every two rows. You may need to make minor adjustments to this ratio in order to pick up the appropriate number of sts.

You should now have 27 (31, 39, 47, 55) sts on your needles.

Set-Up Row (WS): P12 (14, 18, 22, 26), pm, p to end.

Row 1 (RS): K1, ssk, k to 3 sts before m, cdd, rm, k1, pm, k to last 3 sts, k2tog, k1. [4 sts dec]

Row 2 (WS): P all, sm as you come to it.

Rep Rows 1 and 2 until you have 7 sts on your needles. End after completing a WS row. BO all sts knitwise on a RS row. Break yarn, leaving a 6-inch (15-cm) tail.

Top Panel

With the RS of your work facing you, place the 24 (26, 29, 32, 35) Right Side Panel sts on your needles, pick up and knit 15 (17, 21, 25, 29) sts along the upper edge of the Center Back Triangle. Using your LH circular needle, place the 24 (26, 29, 32, 35) Left Side Panel sts on your needles. See Fig. 2.

> Note: The 15 (17, 21, 25, 29) sts you picked up along the top of the Center Back Triangle are your Top Panel sts.

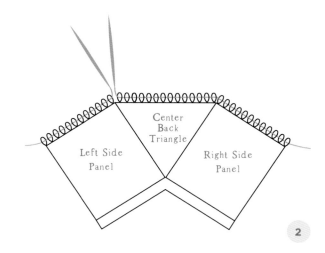

You should now have 63 (69, 79, 89, 99) sts on your needles. You will now begin working short rows to create the Top Panel while simultaneously joining the Top Panel to the Side Panels. Turn your work so that you are ready to work a WS row. On the following row, you will begin working the Top Panel sts on a WS row.

> Note: Check to see if your sts are placed correctly before working the following Set-Up Row. With the WS of the work facing you, you should have 24 (26, 29, 32, 35) sts on your RH needle (these are your Left Side Panel sts) and 39 (43, 50, 57, 64) sts on your LH needle (these are your Top Panel sts and the Right Side Panel sts).

Set-Up Row (WS): Sl1p wyif, p13 (15, 19, 23, 27), p2tog (1 st from the Top Panel with 1 st from the Right Side Panel), turn work. [1 st dec; 62 (68, 78, 84, 98) sts total]

Row 1 (RS): Sl1p wyib, k13 (15, 19, 23, 27), ssk (1 st from the Top Panel with 1 st from the Left Side Panel), turn work. [1 st dec]

Row 2 (WS): Sl1p wyif, p13 (15, 19, 23, 27), p2tog (1 st from the Top Panel with 1 st from the Right Side Panel), turn work. [1 st dec]

Rep rows 1 and 2 until 31 (35, 41, 47, 53) sts remain. End after completing a RS row. You should have 15 (17, 21, 25, 29) Top Panel sts and 8 (9, 10, 11, 12) sts for each Side Panel.

> Note: The following section is designed to create a point at the front of the hat, in the middle of the forehead. If you prefer a straight edge along the front, continue to rep rows 1 and 2 until 15 (17, 21, 25, 29) sts remain. End after completing a RS row. Then work the BO according to the pattern.

Set-Up Row (WS): Sl1p wyif, p6 (7, 9, 11, 13), pm, p1, pm, p6 (7, 9, 11, 13), p2tog (1 st from the Top Panel with 1 st from the Right Side Panel), turn work. [1 st dec; 30 (34, 40, 46, 52) sts total]

Row 3 (RS): Sl1p wyib, k2tog, k4 (5, 7, 9, 11), m1R, sm, k1, sm, m1L, k4 (5, 7, 9, 11), ssk twice (on the second ssk, 1 st from the Top Panel with 1 st from the Left Side Panel), turn work. [1 st dec]

Row 4 (WS): Sl1p wyif, p13 (15, 19, 23, 27), p2tog (1 st from the Top Panel with 1 st from the Right Side Panel), turn work. [1 st dec]

Rep Rows 3 and 4 until 15 (17, 21, 25, 29) sts remain. End after completing a RS row. You should have 15 (17, 21, 25, 29) Top Panel sts. There will be no Side Panel sts remaining.

On a WS row, BO as follows: Sl1p wyif, p1, p2tog, (sl3 sts just worked back to the LH needle, p2, p2tog) rep until 6 sts remain on the needles.

Use the Kitchener Stitch method (page 181) to graft the first 3 sts on your needles to the last 3 sts on your needles. Break yarn, leaving a 6-inch (15-cm) tail.

> Note: You may find that the point of your hat curls up after you have completed the Kitchener Stitch grafting. Properly wet blocking the hat will solve this problem (see the Finishing section). Wearing the hat will also reduce curling.

I-Cord Ties (both worked identically)

Using your DPNs and with the RS of your hat facing you, pick up and knit 3 sts at the bottom front corner of your hat. *Without turning your work, slide these 3 sts from one end of your needle to the other. Place the needle with the live sts in your left hand without turning your work. The working yarn will be coming across the back of your work. Knit these 3 sts again, giving a gentle tug on the first st to tighten the back of the tube you are creating. Rep from * until your i-cord measures approximately 8 (8, 10, 10, 10) inches [20 (20, 25, 25, 25) cm]. BO all sts and break yarn, leaving a 6-inch (15-cm) tail.

Finishing

Weave in all ends. For the best results, be sure to wet block your finished bonnet. Soak the hat in cold water, squeezing to remove air bubbles. Squeeze out the water, but do not wring. Roll the bonnet in a dry towel, burrito-style, and press on it to remove excess water. Place the bonnet on a balloon (inflated to approximately your desired head size) to dry. Use a measuring tape to be sure your bonnet is the correct dimensions.

Backdrop Hat
Skill Level: Adventurous Beginner

My daughters are always on the hunt for thicker, warmer hats. My youngest daughter has been known to wear multiple hats to school, and she is not afraid to mix and match her colors. In that spirit, I created the extra warm Backdrop Hat with two layers of color. The outer layer is knit using self-striping yarn while the inner layer is knit in a solid color. The sweet eyelets in the outer layer provide a peak of the inner layer so that all that lovely knitting time isn't hidden away. The solid yarn creates a perfect backdrop for the outer rainbow of color. As a bonus, this hat is also fully reversible (see photo on page 66).

Construction

This hat is worked seamlessly in the round from the bottom up. After completing the brim, the number of stitches is doubled. Half of the stitches are placed on hold for the outer hat while the inner lining of the hat is completed. Then, the held stitches are placed back on the needles and the outer hat is worked in the round to the crown. The hat lining and the outer hat are joined with a tassel.

Maximum Stitches Used for a Self-Striping Round: 88 (100, 104, 116, 128)

Sizes

Baby (Toddler, Child, Adult M, Adult L)

See the Finished Measurements on page 64 to choose your size.

Yarn

- Fingering weight yarn, Mudpunch Slash Self-Striping Sock
- (80% superwash merino & 20% nylon, 385 yards / 3.8 ounces [352 m / 110 g])
- Sock weight yarn, Lolodidit Guernsey Sport
- (85% merino and 15% mulberry silk, 325 yards / 3.5 ounces [297 m / 100 g])
- Samples shown in "Irresistible Bliss" (MC, self-striping) and "Sh Boom" (CC, blue)
- 1 skein of MC and 1 (1, 1, 2, 2) skeins of CC
- **Main Color:** 110 (125, 165, 205, 235) yards / [100 (114, 151, 187, 215) m]
- **Contrasting Color:** 180 (220, 270, 340, 390) yards / [165 (201, 247, 311, 357) m]

Yarn Notes

This hat was knit using an especially squishy self-striping yarn. This heavy fingering yarn has wonderful warmth and vibrant color. I paired my self-striping yarn with a high-contrast solid so that it would shine through the eyelets of the outer hat.

Needles

US 4 (3.5 mm) and US 3 (3.25 mm) 16-inch (40-cm) circular needles (length as appropriate for your size), or as required to meet gauge

DPNs in the LARGER size

Gauge

22 stitches and 30 rounds = 4 inches (10 cm) in stockinette stitch on LARGER needles after blocking

Notions

- 4 stitch markers
- Scissors
- Scrap yarn
- Tapestry needle
- Tape measure

Finished Measurements

I recommend knitting this pattern with zero ease. Samples shown in Child size.

A. **Circumference:** 16 (18.25, 19, 21, 23.25) inches / [40.5 (46.5, 48.5, 53.5, 59) cm]

B. **Brim Length (unfolded):** 3 (4, 4, 5, 5) inches / [7.5 (10, 10, 12.5, 12.5) cm]

C. **Body Length:** 3.5 (4, 4.5, 5.5, 5.5) inches / [9 (10, 11.5, 14, 14) cm]

D. **Crown Length:** 1.5 (1.75, 1.75, 2, 2.25) inches / [3.5 (4.5, 4.5, 5, 5.5) cm]

E. **Total Length:** 8 (9.75, 10.25, 12.5, 12.75) inches / [20.5 (25, 26, 32, 32.5) cm]

Abbreviations	
BOR	beginning of round
CC	contrast color
CO	cast on
dec	decrease
DPNs	double pointed needles
k	knit
kfb	knit into the front and back of one stitch
k2tog	knit two together
LH	left-hand
m	marker
MC	main color
p	purl
pm	place marker
p2tog	purl two together
rep	repeat
sl1p	slip one purlwise
sm	slip marker
ssk	slip, slip, knit
ssp	slip, slip, purl
st(s)	stitch(es)
yo	yarn over

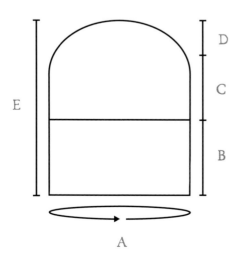

Pattern

Brim

Using SMALLER circular needles and CC, CO 88 (100, 104, 116, 128) sts. Place a BOR marker and join to work in the round.

Work 2x2 ribbing (k2, p2) until your work measures 3 (4, 4, 5, 5) inches [7.5 (10, 10, 12.5, 12.5) cm] from the CO edge.

Division

In this section, you will double the number of sts on your needles. Then you will place half of these sts on hold.

Set-Up Round: Kfb to end. [88 (100, 104, 116, 128) sts inc; 176 (200, 208, 232, 256) sts total]

In the following round, every other st will be placed on a piece of scrap yarn. These will be the odd-numbered sts. All even-numbered sts will stay on your needles.

Note: When you place sts onto scrap yarn, make sure that these sts are held in front, while the sts that remain on the needles are in back. The sts held on scrap yarn are the first round of the Outer Hat.

Division Round: (Sl1p onto a piece of scrap yarn, Sl1p) rep to end.

You now have 88 (100, 104, 116, 128) sts on your needles. These sts are your Hat Lining sts. You have 88 (100, 104, 116, 128) sts on a piece of scrap yarn. These are your Outer Hat sts.

Hat Lining

Note: You will find that while working the first rounds of your Hat Lining, the slipped sts will become quite large. This is normal. When you begin the Outer Hat, you can adjust the tension of these sts. For now, there is no need to alter these stretched-out sts.

Change to LARGER needles. Work in stockinette stitch (k every round) until your hat measures 6.5 (8, 8.5, 10.5, 10.5) inches [16.5 (20.5, 21.5, 26.5, 26.5) cm] from the CO edge.

Crown Set-Up Round: [K22 (25, 26, 29, 32), pm] 3 times, k22 (25, 26, 29, 32).

Decrease Round: (Ssp, k to 3 sts before m, p2tog, p1, sm) 4 times. [8 sts dec]

Rep Decrease Round an additional 8 (10, 10, 12, 13) times [16 (12, 16, 12, 16) sts total]. Change to DPNs once the crown becomes too small for your circular needles.

Baby, Child and Adult L only: (Ssp, k2, sm) 4 times. [4 sts dec; 12 (-, 12, -, 12) sts total]

All sizes: (Ssp, k1) 4 times. [4 sts dec; 8 sts total]

Break yarn, leaving a 24-inch (61-cm) tail. Using a tapestry needle, pull yarn through 8 remaining live sts and pull the hole closed.

Do not weave in the end at the top of the Hat Lining.

Note: If you are not planning to work a tassel at the top of your hat, weave in the end at the top of your Hat Lining.

Outer Hat

Place 88 (100, 104, 116, 128) held sts on your LARGER circular needles.

Note: As you place the Outer Hat sts onto your needles, the sts that were stretched while working the Hat Lining should return to their normal size. If you find that either the Hat Lining sts or the Outer Hat sts need to be adjusted further, I recommend waiting until you have finished knitting the Outer Hat.

Join your MC and place a BOR marker. Knit every round until you reach the color change of your self-striping yarn.

Note: I worked two full stripes in the MC yarn before working the eyelets because the stripes were quite narrow. You can decide if you want to work the eyelets between every stripe, every other stripe, every third stripe, etc. Keep in mind that the color change will most certainly not be at the beginning of the round. Don't worry! When you reach the color change, simply start working the Eyelet Round on the first stitch of the new color in your striping sequence, then work in stockinette until you reach the BOR marker.

In the following round, you will be working a double yarn over. In order to do this, simply wrap the yarn for the first yarn over and then repeat. This will create a single loop of yarn that is wrapped twice around the needle to create a larger eyelet opening.

Eyelet Round 1: (K2tog, yo twice) 44 (50, 52, 58, 64) times.

Eyelet Round 2: (K1, knit the first yo, drop the second yo off your needles without working it) 44 (50, 52, 58, 64) times.

Knit until you reach the next color change in your striping sequence. Rep this sequence (Eyelet Rounds 1 and 2 and stockinette stitch) until your hat measures 6.5 (8, 8.5, 10.5, 10.5) inches [16.5 (20.5, 21.5, 26.5, 26.5) cm] from the CO edge. End after working at least one complete stockinette round.

Note: If you are knitting this pattern with a solid yarn instead of a self-striping yarn, I recommend knitting four rounds, then working the Eyelet Rounds. Rep these six rounds until you reach your target length.

Before working the crown decreases, weave in the MC end at the brim of the hat.

Crown Set-Up Round: [K22 (25, 26, 29, 32), pm] 3 times, k22 (25, 26, 29, 32).

Creating a Tassel

Create a tassel using the length of yarn left at the top of the hat lining. Pull this length of yarn through the hole at the top of the Outer Hat. Pull the hole closed. Place the 24-inch (61-cm) tail of CC on your tapestry needle.

Step 1: Bring the tapestry needle through the tip of the hat. To secure the Hat Lining to the Outer Hat, make sure that the needle passes through the lining as well.

Step 2: Bring a loop of yarn over your index finger and back through the tip of the hat.

Step 3: Continue to bring the tapestry needle back through the tip of the hat, catching the loops with your index finger until you have completed the desired number of loops.

Step 4: Wrap the yarn two to three times tightly around the loops near the tip of the hat.

Step 5: Insert the tapestry needle from bottom to top through the center of the tassel.

Step 6: Trim the tassel according to your taste.

Flip your hat inside out and repeat this process to create a tassel on the Lining side of your hat using the length of MC yarn.

Decrease Round: (K2tog, k to 3 sts before m, ssk, k1, sm) 4 times. [8 sts dec]

Rep Decrease Round an additional 8 (10, 10, 12, 13) times [16 (12, 16, 12, 16) sts total]. Change to DPNs once the crown becomes too small for your circular needles.

Baby, Child & Adult L only: (K2tog, k2, sm) 4 times. [4 sts dec; 12 (-, 12, -, 12) sts total]

All sizes: (K2tog, k1) 4 times. [4 sts dec; 8 sts total]

Break yarn, leaving a 24-inch (61-cm) tail. Using a tapestry needle, pull yarn through 8 remaining live sts. Before you pull the hole at the top of the Outer Hat closed, use the following instructions to attach the Hat Lining to the Outer Hat:

Finishing

Weave in all remaining ends. Double check the tension of the sts at the Division for the Hat Lining and Outer Hat. Look for sts that appear to be too small. Insert the tip of your knitting needle into these small sts and pull the needle through so that small sts adjust to fit the needle. This will pull both the smaller sts and larger sts into their proper size. Once finished, be sure to wet block your finished hat. Soak the hat in cold water, squeezing to remove air bubbles. Squeeze out the water, but do not wring. Roll the hat in a dry towel, burrito-style, and press on it to remove excess water. Place the hat on a balloon (inflated to approximately your desired head size) to dry. Use a measuring tape to be sure your hat is the correct dimensions.

Gallivant Hat

Skill Level: Adventurous Beginner

Over a decade ago, I knit an earflap hat for my husband that he still wears to this day. One particularly cold winter, he told me that if he had to choose one article of clothing to wear in a snowstorm, it would be that hat. While I wouldn't recommend gallivanting around in the snow with nothing but your hat, I can wholeheartedly recommend earflaps on your next hat. A good earflap hat will keep your head and your neck warm. The Gallivant Hat was designed to showcase the full potential of your self-striping yarn. By changing the texture of your stitches, direction of your stripes and length of your rows and rounds, you will see your yarn transform as you create your new favorite winter accessory.

Construction

This hat is knit seamlessly from the left earflap to the right earflap. Then the body of the hat is picked up along the edge of the brim and knit in the round to the crown.

Maximum Stitches Used for a Self-Striping Round: 72 (76, 84, 92)

Sizes

Toddler (Child, Adult S/M, Adult L)

See the Finished Measurements on page 70 to choose your size.

Yarn

- Worsted weight yarn, Must Stash Sweater Weather
- (100% merino, 220 yards / 3.5 ounces [201 m / 100 g])
- Samples shown in "Denali"
- 1 skein
- 105 (135, 175, 200) yards / [96 (124, 160, 183) m]

Yarn Notes

I used a self-striping yarn that has a beautiful gradient effect. Gradient stripes, with their gradual color changes, are particularly useful when working with a self-striping yarn in garter stitch.

Needles

US 8 (5 mm) 16-inch (40-cm) circular needles, or as required to meet gauge

DPNs in the same size

Gauge

16 stitches and 24 rounds = 4 inches (10 cm) in stockinette stitch after blocking

16 stitches and 36 rounds = 4 inches (10 cm) in garter stitch after blocking

Notions

- 9 stitch markers
- Scissors
- Tapestry needle
- Tape measure

Finished Measurements

I recommend knitting this pattern with zero ease. Sample shown in the Adult L. Choose a size according to your head circumference. If you are between sizes, choose the larger of the two sizes.

A. **Circumference:** 18 (19, 21, 23) inches / [46 (48.5, 53.5, 58.5) cm]

B. **Brim Length:** 2.25 (2.5, 2.75, 3) inches / [6 (6.5, 7, 7.5) cm]

C. **Body Length:** 2.5 (3, 3.5, 3.5) inches / [6 (7.5, 9, 9) cm]

D. **Crown Length:** 2 (2, 2.25, 2.5) inches / [5 (5, 5.5, 6.5) cm]

E. **Earflap Length:** 2.25 (2.75, 3.25, 3.75) inches / [6 (7, 8, 9.5) cm]

F. **Total Length:** 6.75 (7.5, 8.75, 9) inches / [17 (19, 21.5, 23) cm]

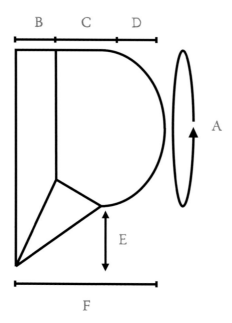

Abbreviations	
BO	bind off
BOR	beginning of round
CO	cast on
dec	decrease
DPNs	double pointed needles
inc	increase
k	knit
k2tog	knit two together
LH	left-hand
m	marker
m1L	make one left
m1R	make one right
p	purl
pm	place marker
rep	repeat
RS	right side
sl1p	slip one purlwise
sm	slip marker
ssk	slip, slip, knit
st(s)	stitch(es)
WS	wrong side
wyif	with yarn in front

Pattern

Left Earflap

Note: The Left Earflap refers to the LH side of the hat as worn. That is, when your hat is complete, this earflap will be on the left side of your head. All references to "left" and "right" throughout the pattern will be "as worn."

CO 3 sts.

Set-Up Row (WS): Sl1p wyif, pm, p1, pm, k1.

Row 1 (RS): Sl1p wyif, m1R, sm, k1, sm, m1L, k1. [2 sts inc; 5 sts total]

Row 2 (WS): Sl1p wyif, k1, sm, p1, sm, k2.

Row 3 (RS): Sl1p wyif, k to m, m1R, sm, k1, sm, k to end. [1 st inc; 6 sts total]

Row 4 (WS): Sl1p wyif, k to m, sm, p1, sm, k to end.

Row 5 (RS): Sl1p wyif, k to m, m1R, sm, k1, sm, m1L, k to end. [2 sts inc; 8 sts total]

Row 6 (WS): Sl1p wyif, k to m, sm, p1, sm, k to end.

Rep Rows 3–6 an additional 6 (7, 8, 9) times. Rep Rows 3 and 4 once more. You should have a total of 27 (30, 33, 36) sts on your needles. You should have 17 (19, 21, 23) sts before the first st marker, 1 st between the markers, and 9 (10, 11, 12) sts after the second st marker.

In the following row, remove the markers as you come to them.

Division Row (RS): BO 17 (19, 21, 23), k to end.

You should now have 10 (11, 12, 13) sts on your needles.

Brim

Next Row (WS): Sl1p wyif, k to end.

Garter Row 1 (RS): Sl1p wyif, k to end.

Garter Row 2 (WS): Sl1p wyif, k to end.

Rep Garter Rows 1 and 2 an additional 36 (36, 40, 44) times, after completing a WS row. This will create 37 (37, 41, 45) garter ridges and 37 (37, 41, 45) slipped sts along the edge of the Brim.

Right Earflap

With the RS facing you, use the Cable cast on method to CO 17 (19, 21, 23) sts to your LH needle (in front of the sts worked in the last Garter Row at the end of the Brim). You will now have 27 (30, 33, 36) sts on your needles, 17 (19, 21, 23) new CO sts and the original 10 (11, 12, 13) Brim sts.

Note: If the Cable cast on method is new to you, see page 177 for more information on how to work this cast on.

Row 1 (RS): K17 (19, 21, 23), pm, k1, pm, k9 (10, 11, 12).

Row 2 (WS): Sl1p wyif, k to m, sm, p1, sm, k to end.

Row 3 (RS): Sl1p wyif, k to 2 sts before m, ssk, sm, k1, sm, k2tog, k to end. [2 sts dec; 25 (28, 31, 34) sts total]

Row 4 (WS): Sl1p wyif, k to m, sm, p1, sm, k to end.

Row 5 (RS): Sl1p wyif, k to 2 sts before m, ssk, sm, k1, sm, k to end. [1 st dec; 24 (27, 30, 33) sts total]

Row 6 (WS): Sl1p wyif, k to m, sm, p1, sm, k to end.

Rep Rows 3–6 an additional 6 (7, 8, 9) times [6 sts total]. Rep Rows 3 and 4 once more [2 st dec; 4 sts total].

Row 7 (RS): Ssk, sm, k1, sm, k to end. [1 st dec; 3 sts total]

Row 8 (WS): Sl1p wyif, sm, p1, sm, k1.

You should have a total of 3 sts on your needles. BO all sts knitwise on a RS row. Break yarn, leaving a 6-inch (15-cm) tail.

Hat Body

Beginning at the BO edge of the Left Earflap, pick up and knit 17 (19, 21, 23) sts along the BO edge of the Left Earflap, 38 (38, 42, 46) sts along the edge of the Brim, and 17 (19, 21, 23) sts along the CO edge of the Right Earflap (see Fig. 1 below). You should now have 72 (76, 84, 92) sts on your needles. Place a BOR marker and join to work in the round.

Sts for Body of the hat are picked up along the RED line.

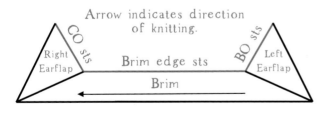

Arrow indicates direction of knitting.

Work in stockinette stitch (k every round) until your hat measures 4.75 (5.5, 6.25, 6.5) inches [12 (14, 16, 16.5) cm] from the edge of the brim (you will be measuring both the garter Brim and the stockinette Hat Body together).

Crown

In this section, you will be decreasing for the crown of the hat. Change to DPNs once the crown becomes too small for your circular needles.

Toddler Set-Up Round: (K8, pm) 8 times, k8.

Child Set-Up Round: (K7, k2tog, pm, k8, pm) 4 times, k8. [4 sts dec; 72 sts total]

Adult S/M Set-Up Round: [(K9, pm) 2 times, K8, k2tog, pm] 2 times, (K9, pm) 2 times, K8, k2tog. [3 sts dec; 81 sts total]

Adult L Set-Up Round: [(K10, pm) 3 times, K9, k2tog, pm] 2 times, k10. [2 sts dec; 90 sts total]

Next Round: K all.

Round 1: (K to 2 sts before m, k2tog, sm) 9 times. [9 sts dec; 63 (63, 72, 81) sts total]

Round 2: (K to m, sm) 9 times.

Rep Rounds 1 and 2 an additional 2 (2, 3, 3) times. [45 (45, 45, 54) sts total]

Round 3: (K to 2 sts before m, k2tog, sm) 9 times. [9 sts dec; 36 (36, 36, 45) sts total]

Rep Round 3 an additional 3 (3, 3, 4) times. [9 sts total]

Break yarn, leaving a 6-inch (15-cm) tail. Using a tapestry needle, pull yarn through 9 remaining live sts and pull the hole closed.

Finishing

Weave in all remaining ends. For the best results, be sure to wet block your finished hat. Soak the hat in cold water, squeezing to remove air bubbles. Squeeze out the water, but do not wring. Roll the hat in a dry towel, burrito-style, and press on it to remove excess water. Place the hat on a balloon (inflated to approximately your desired head size) to dry. Use a measuring tape to be sure your hat is the correct dimensions.

stash-Busting

Cowls That Dazzle

Cowls are the perfect way to bust through your stash fast! They make great gifts, and if you keep them, they add sparkle to your wardrobe. Small and light, these projects are the perfect opportunity to use your best and brightest self-striping yarn. A happy rainbow cowl peeking out the top of your coat adds a pop of cheer to even the dreariest winter day.

In these pages, we will explore the most exciting stitches to work when knitting with self-striping yarn. Using slipped stitches, dip stitches, a touch of lace and so much more, we will add texture and depth to your stripes. Throughout this chapter, you will find projects that use up all the bits and bobs hanging around in your stash. You can knit up the minis leftover from larger projects in the Rainbow Blowout Cowl (page 91) while you try not one or two, but five great stitches for self-striping yarn. Do you need a two-skein project? Enjoy the vertical lines created using slipped stitches in the Encompassing Cowl (page 87). Want a relaxing, repetitive stitch for a really spectacular skein of self-striping? Try the Wave at the Rainbow Cowl (page 77). Before you know it, you will have a stack of fabulous gifts or accessories and a sizable dent in your stash.

Wave at the Rainbow Cowl

Skill Level: Beginner

Cowls are like the sprinkles on a cupcake. They add a little bit of extra oomph that makes everything look bright and happy. The Wave at the Rainbow Cowl is the perfect place to showcase a really spectacular skein of yarn and give your outfit some extra brightness. The regular increases and decreases in this cowl bend the stripes to create a lovely wave effect without distracting from the beauty of the yarn. You will be shocked at how quickly this cowl flies off the needles.

Construction
This pattern is knit seamlessly in the round from end to end.

Maximum Stitches Used for a Self-Striping Round: 160

Sizes
One Size

See the Finished Measurements on page 78.

Yarn
- Fingering weight yarn, Fab Funky Fibres
- (75% superwash merino and 25% nylon, 370 yards / 2.8 ounces [338 m / 80 g])
- Sample shown in "Walking on Rainbows" (MC) and "Charcoal" (CC)
- 1 skein of MC and 1 skein of CC
- **Main Color:** 464 yards (424 m)
- **Contrasting Color:** 70 yards (64 m)

Yarn Notes
This pattern was knit using a particularly exciting yarn that has no color repeats. Every color in the self-striping yarn is used only once, so the color run is the entire skein.

Needles
US 6 (4 mm) 24-inch (60-cm) circular needles, or as required to meet gauge

US 5 (3.5 mm) 24-inch (60-cm) circular needles

Gauge
28 stitches and 34 rounds = 4 inches (10 cm) in wave pattern after blocking on LARGER needles

Notions
- 1 stitch marker
- Scissors
- Tapestry needle
- Tape measure

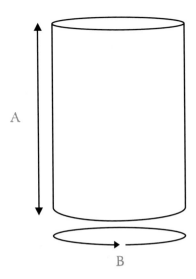

A

B

Finished Measurements
A. **Length:** 16.5 inches (41.5 cm)
B. **Circumference:** 23 inches (57.5 cm)

Abbreviations	
BOR	beginning of round
CC	contrasting color
CO	cast on
k	knit
k2tog	knit two together
m	marker
MC	main color
m1L	make one left
m1R	make one right
p	purl
rep	repeat
ssk	slip, slip, knit
st(s)	stitch(es)
wyib	with yarn in back

Pattern

Using SMALLER needles and CC, CO 160 sts. Place a BOR marker and join to work in the round.

Work 1x1 ribbing (k1, p1) until your work measures 1.5 inches (4 cm). Break yarn, leaving a 6-inch (15-cm) tail.

Change to LARGER needles and join MC. In the following round, you will move the BOR marker one st to the left at the end of the round.

Set-Up Round: Knit to end of round, remove BOR m, sl1p wyib, replace BOR m.

Rep Rounds 1–18 of the Wave at the Rainbow chart on page 79 until your work measures approximately 15 inches (37.5 cm) or your desired length.

K one round. Break yarn, leaving a 6-inch (15-cm) tail.

> Note: If you are trying to maximize your yardage, you don't have to finish on Round 18. To create a clean, beautifully finished cowl, I recommend ending after completing either Round 9 or Round 18. Just remember to leave enough yardage to work the final knit round.

Change to SMALLER needles and join CC.

K one round.

Work 1x1 ribbing (k1, p1) until ribbing measures 1.5 inches (4 cm). BO all sts in pattern. Break yarn, leaving a 6-inch (15-cm) tail.

Finishing

Weave in all ends. For the best results, be sure to wet block your finished cowl. Soak the cowl in cold water, squeezing to remove air bubbles. Squeeze out the water, but do not wring. Roll the cowl in a dry towel, burrito-style, and press on it to remove excess water. Lay the cowl flat to dry, using a measuring tape to be sure it is laid out with the correct dimensions.

Written Instructions for Chart

Round 1: (M1L, k8, k2tog) 16 times.

Round 2: (K1, m1L, k7, k2tog) 16 times.

Round 3: (K2, m1L, k6, k2tog) 16 times.

Round 4: (K3, m1L, k5, k2tog) 16 times.

Round 5: (K4, m1L, k4, k2tog) 16 times.

Round 6: (K5, m1L, k3, k2tog) 16 times.

Round 7: (K6, m1L, k2, k2tog) 16 times.

Round 8: (K7, m1L, k1, k2tog) 16 times.

Round 9: (K8, m1L, k2tog) 16 times.

Round 10: (Ssk, k8, m1R) 16 times.

Round 11: (Ssk, k7, m1R, k1) 16 times.

Round 12: (Ssk, k6, m1R, k2) 16 times.

Round 13: (Ssk, k5, m1R, k3) 16 times.

Round 14: (Ssk, k4, m1R, k4) 16 times.

Round 15: (Ssk, k3, m1R, k5) 16 times.

Round 16: (Ssk, k2, m1R, k6) 16 times.

Round 17: (Ssk, k1, m1R, k7) 16 times.

Round 18: (Ssk, m1R, k8) 16 times.

Chart Instructions

To work charts, begin at the bottom right corner and work right to left.

Key	
□	knit
◺	ssk
◹	k2tog
m1L symbol	m1L
m1R symbol	m1R

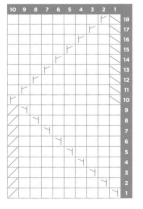

Slippery Cowl

Skill Level: Adventurous Beginner

Most of the self-striping yarns that I have hiding in my stash were dyed to be socks. They make narrow little stripes, and they are spectacular for small projects like mittens and, well, socks. That's wonderful, but I recently had a chat with my yarn stash, and we decided that sometimes sock yarn just doesn't want to be socks. This yarn in particular wanted to be a cowl, so I set about making its dreams come true. The Slippery Cowl was designed to keep the rows short so that you can use narrow stripes that were meant for socks on your neck. Knit in three seamless panels, this cowl uses vertical and horizontal stripes in combination with slipped stitches to draw lines that slip and slide in all directions. Go have a chat with your stash. I bet there's a skein in there that wants to be a cowl.

Construction

This cowl begins by working the Center Panel flat. After binding off the top of the Center Panel, the Left Panel is picked up and knit to the back of the neck. Next, the Right Panel is picked up and knit to the back of the neck. Finally, the Left and Right Panels are joined by working a three-needle bind off (see page 180). For a detailed schematic of the construction of the body of this cowl, see Fig. 1 below.

Maximum Stitches Used for a Self-Striping Row: 87

Sizes

One Size

See the Finished Measurements on page 82.

Yarn

- Fingering weight yarn, Quaere Fibers
- (75% superwash merino and 25% nylon, 463 yards / 3.5 ounces [423 m / 100 g])
- Samples shown in "Happy Go Lucky"
- 1 skein
- 375 yards (343 m)

Yarn Notes

This cowl was knit using a truly exciting skein of yarn with a 40-row repeat. This pattern allowed me to show every stripe in this beautiful skein.

Needles

US 3 (3.25 mm) 24-inch (60-cm) circular needles, or as required to meet gauge

Three-needle bind off shown in RED.
Arrows indicate directions of knitting.

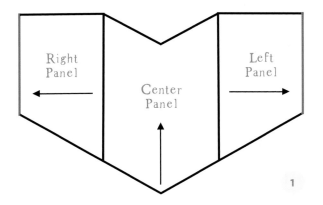

Right Panel

Left Panel

Center Panel

1

Gauge

30 stitches and 40 rows = 4 inches (10 cm) in Slipped Stitch Motif after blocking

Notions

- 2 stitch markers
- Scissors
- Scrap yarn
- Tapestry needle
- Tape measure

Finished Measurements

A. **Circumference:** 21 inches (52.5 cm)

B. **Front Length:** 16 inches (40.5 cm)

C. **Back Length:** 6.75 inches (17 cm)

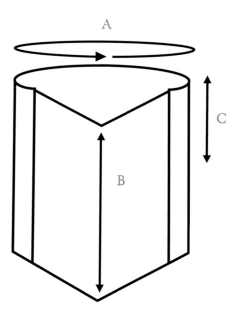

Abbreviations	
BO	bind off
CO	cast on
cdd	central double decrease
dec	decrease
k	knit
k2tog	knit two together
LH	left-hand
m	marker
m1L	make one left
m1R	make one right
p	purl
pm	place marker
rep	repeat
RH	right-hand
RS	right side
sl1k	slip one knitwise
sl1p	slip one purlwise
sm	slip marker
ssk	slip, slip, knit
st(s)	stitch(es)
WS	wrong side
wyib	with yarn in back
wyif	with yarn in front

Pattern

Center Panel

CO 59 sts.

Set-Up Row (WS): (P1, k1) rep to last st, p1.

Row 1 (RS): (K1, p1) rep to last st, k1.

Row 2 (WS): (P1, k1) rep to last st, p1

Rep Rows 1 and 2 an additional three times.

Row 3 (RS): K2, m1L, k1, (sl1p wyib, k3) 6 times, sl1p wyib, cdd, sl1p wyib, (k3, sl1p wyib) 6 times, k1, m1R, k2.

Row 4 (WS): P4, (sl1p wyif, p3) 6 times, sl3p wyif, (p3, sl1p wyif) 6 times, p4.

Row 5 (RS): K2, m1L, k2, (sl1p wyib, k3) 6 times, cdd, (k3, sl1p wyib) 6 times, k2, m1R, k2.

Row 6 (WS): P29, sl1p wyif, p29.

Row 7 (RS): K2, m1L, (k3, sl1p wyib) 6 times, k2, cdd, k2, (sl1p wyib, k3) 6 times, m1R, k2.

Row 8 (WS): P2, (sl1p wyif, p3) 6 times, sl1p wyif, p2, sl1p wyif, p2, sl1p wyif, (p3, sl1p wyif) 6 times, p2.

Row 9 (RS): K2, m1L, (sl1p wyib, k3) 6 times, sl1p wyib, k1, cdd, k1, sl1p wyib, (k3, sl1p wyib) 6 times, m1R, k2.

Row 10 (WS): P29, sl1p wyif, p29.

Rep Rows 3–10 until your work measures approximately 14.5 inches (36 cm). End after completing Row 6. You are now ready for a RS row.

Row 11 (RS): (K1, p1) rep to last st, k1.

Row 12 (WS): (P1, k1) rep to last st, p1.

Rep Rows 11 and 12 an additional three times. BO all sts in pattern on a RS row.

Note: The top edge of this cowl is intended to be rolled in at the neck so that the WS of the fabric is not visible. I do not recommend using a stretchy BO along the top edge of the Center Panel. This will create a loose, less structured upper edge.

I recommend blocking your Center Panel before moving on to the Left Panel. This will help you achieve your target measurements when you complete your cowl. After blocking, the Center Panel will be approximately 7.5 inches (19 cm) wide and 16 inches (40 cm) long. The front length is not as critical to the fit of the cowl. However, if the Center Panel is significantly wider or narrower than this target length, it will change the final circumference of your cowl.

Break yarn, leaving a 6-inch (15-cm) tail.

Left Panel

Note: The Left Panel refers to the LH side of the cowl as worn. That is, when your cowl is complete, this panel will be worn on your left shoulder.

In this section, you will be picking up sts along the edge of the Center Panel.

Lay the Center Panel flat in front of you with the RS facing up. The side edge that you will pick up along should be facing away from you. The CO edge will be at the right end and the BO edge will be at the left end. Beginning at the ribbing edge near the CO, pick up and knit 87 sts along the edge of the Center Panel.

Note: You will be picking up approximately 3 sts for every four rows. You may need to make minor adjustments to this ratio in order to pick up the appropriate number of sts.

Set-Up Row (WS): Sl1p wyif, (k1, p1) 3 times, k1, pm, (p3, sl1p wyif) 17 times, p3, pm, (k1, p1) 4 times.

Row 1 (RS): Sl1k wyib, (p1, k1) 3 times, p1, sm, ssk, k1, (sl1p wyib, k3) rep to m, sm, (p1, k1) 4 times. [1 st dec; 86 sts total]

Row 2 (WS): Sl1p wyif, (k1, p1) 3 times, k1, sm, (p3, sl1p wyif) rep to 2 sts before m, p2, sm, (k1, p1) 4 times.

Row 3 (RS): Sl1k wyib, (p1, k1) 3 times, p1, sm, ssk, k to m, sm, (p1, k1) 4 times. [1 st dec; 85 sts total]

Row 4 (WS): Sl1p wyif, (k1, p1) 3 times, k1, sm, (p3, sl1p wyif) rep to 1 st before m, p1, sm, (k1, p1) 4 times.

Row 5 (RS): Sl1k wyib, (p1, k1) 3 times, p1, sm, ssk, (k3, sl1p wyib) rep to 3 sts before m, k3, sm, (p1, k1) 4 times. [1 st dec; 84 sts total]

Row 6 (WS): Sl1p wyif, (k1, p1) 3 times, k1, sm, (p3, sl1p wyif) rep to 4 sts before m, p4, sm, (k1, p1) 4 times.

Row 7 (RS): Sl1k wyib, (p1, k1) 3 times, p1, sm, ssk, k to m, sm, (p1, k1) 4 times. [1 st dec; 83 sts total]

Row 8 (WS): Sl1p wyif, (k1, p1) 3 times, k1, sm, (p3, sl1p wyif) rep to 3 sts before m, p3, sm, (k1, p1) 4 times.

Row 9 (RS): Sl1k wyib, (p1, k1) 3 times, p1, sm, ssk, k1, (sl1p wyib, k3) rep to m, sm, (p1, k1) 4 times. [1 st dec; 82 sts total]

Row 10 (WS): Sl1p wyif, (k1, p1) 3 times, k1, sm, (p3, sl1p wyif) rep to 2 sts before m, p2, sm, (k1, p1) 4 times.

Rep Rows 3–10 an additional eight times. [50 sts]

Note: Your Left Panel should measure approximately 6.75 inches (17 cm) from the edge of the Center Panel. If your row gauge does not match the pattern, I recommend working Rows 3–10 until you reach this length. End after completing any WS row in the repeat. This will mean that you will have a different number of sts on your needles for the three-needle bind off and that your back-of-the-neck measurement will be different. Don't worry! It is more important to focus on the circumference of your cowl in order to achieve a good fit.

Break yarn, leaving a 6-inch (15-cm) tail. Place all sts onto a piece of scrap yarn.

Right Panel

Note: The Right Panel refers to the RH side of the cowl as worn. That is, when your cowl is complete, this panel will be worn on your right shoulder.

In this section, you will be picking up sts along the edge of the Center Panel, opposite of the Left Panel.

Lay the Center Panel flat in front of you with the RS facing up. The side edge that you will pick up along should be facing away from you, and the Left Panel will be toward you. The CO edge of the Center Panel will be at the left end, and the BO edge will be at the right end. Beginning at the ribbing edge near the BO, pick up and knit 87 sts along the edge of the Center Panel.

Set-Up Row (WS): Sl1p wyif, (k1, p1) 3 times, k1, pm, (p3, sl1p wyif) 17 times, p3, pm, (k1, p1) 4 times.

Row 1 (RS): Sl1k wyib, (p1, k1) 3 times, p1, sm, (k3, sl1p wyib) rep to 3 sts before m, k1, k2tog, sm, (p1, k1) 4 times. [1 st dec; 86 sts total]

Row 2 (WS): Sl1p wyif, (k1, p1) 3 times, k1, sm, p2, (sl1p wyif, p3) rep to m, sm, (k1, p1) 4 times.

Row 3 (RS): Sl1k wyib, (p1, k1) 3 times, p1, sm, k to 2 sts before m, k2tog, sm, (p1, k1) 4 times. [1 st dec; 85 sts total]

Row 4 (WS): Sl1p wyif, (k1, p1) 3 times, k1, sm, p1, (sl1p wyif, p3) rep to m, sm, (k1, p1) 4 times.

Row 5 (RS): Sl1k wyib, (p1, k1) 3 times, p1, sm, (k3, sl1p wyib) rep to 5 sts before m, k3, k2tog, sm, (p1, k1) 4 times. [1 st dec; 84 sts total]

Row 6 (WS): Sl1p wyif, (k1, p1) 3 times, k1, sm, p4, (sl1p wyif, p3) rep to m, sm, (k1, p1) 4 times.

Row 7 (RS): Sl1k wyib, (p1, k1) 3 times, p1, sm, k to 2 sts before m, k2tog, sm, (p1, k1) 4 times. [1 st dec; 83 sts total]

Row 8 (WS): Sl1p wyif, (k1, p1) 3 times, k1, sm, p3, (sl1p wyif, p3) rep to m, sm, (k1, p1) 4 times.

Row 9 (RS): Sl1k wyib, (p1, k1) 3 times, p1, sm, (k3, sl1p wyib) rep to 3 sts before m, k1, k2tog, sm, (p1, k1) 4 times. [1 st dec; 82 sts total]

Row 10 (WS): Sl1p wyif, (k1, p1) 3 times, k1, sm, p2, (sl1p wyif, p3) rep to m, sm, (k1, p1) 4 times.

Rep Rows 3–10 an additional eight times. [50 sts]

Note: If you adjusted the number of rows in the Left Panel, remember to make the same adjustment here. End when you have the same number of sts on your needles as you have on hold for your Left Panel. End after completing a WS row.

Break yarn, leaving a 24-inch (61-cm) tail. Place held Left Panel on your needles. With the RS held together, align the Left Panel and Right Panel sts. Use a third needle to join the Left Panel and Right Panel sts using a three-needle bind off (see page 180).

Finishing

Weave in all ends. For the best results, be sure to wet block your finished cowl. Soak the cowl in cold water, squeezing to remove air bubbles. Squeeze out the water, but do not wring. Roll the cowl in a dry towel, burrito-style, and press on it to remove excess water. Lay the cowl flat to dry, using a measuring tape to be sure it is laid out with the correct dimensions.

Encompassing Cowl
Skill Level: Adventurous Beginner

Here's the trouble with feet. They are small. Okay, not my feet. I have big feet, but other people have small feet, and self-striping sock yarn is designed for feet. That often means the yarn has small stripes, and if you are knitting a cowl, small stripes can spell trouble. Small stripes are tricky to use in cowls because necks are larger than feet. Well, when your stripes are small, this is how you stretch a stripe. The Encompassing Cowl uses a nifty trick. By alternating between the self-striping yarn and a contrasting color every other round, the stripes from the self-striping yarn look wider. Suddenly, sock yarn with narrow stripes works perfectly for humans with necks larger than their feet. Ta-da! It's magic.

Construction
This cowl is worked seamlessly in the round from the top down. After working the top hem and the cowl body, the bottom hem is split and the back and front are worked flat.

Maximum Stitches Used for a Self-Striping Round: 120

Yarn Notes
I knit this cowl using a self-striping yarn with narrow stripes, originally intended for knitting socks. Alternating between a solid and a self-striping yarn is a wonderful way to stretch your stripes in order to use your beautiful self-striping yarn in projects with a larger circumference.

Sizes
One Size

See the Finished Measurements on page 88.

Needles
US 5 (3.75 mm) 16-inch (40-cm) circular needles, or as required to meet gauge

US 3 (3.25 mm) 16-inch (40-cm) circular needles, or as required to meet gauge

Yarn
- Fingering weight yarn, Valkyrie Fibers Matte Sock
- (75% superwash merino and 25% nylon, 463 yards / 100g)
- Samples shown in "I Was Drunk, It Was Comic-Con" (MC, self-striping) and "Tiniest Umbrella" (CC, brown)
- 1 skein of MC and 1 mini skein of CC
- **Main Color:** 260 yards (238 m)
- **Contrasting Color:** 200 yards (183 m)

Gauge
24 stitches and 32 rows = 4 inches (10 cm) in stockinette stitch in the round on LARGER needles after blocking

Notions
- 1 stitch marker
- Scissors
- Scrap yarn
- Tapestry needle
- Tape measure

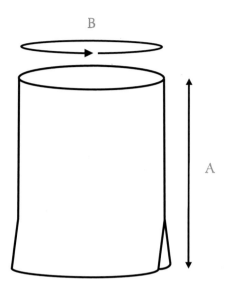

Abbreviations	
BO	bind off
BOR	beginning of round
CC	contrasting color
CO	cast on
k	knit
m	marker
MC	main color
p	purl
rep	repeat
RH	right-hand
sl1k	slip one knitwise
sl1p	slip one purlwise
st(s)	stitch(es)
wyib	with yarn in back
wyif	with yarn in front

Pattern

Top Hem

Using SMALLER needles and CC, CO 120 sts. Place the BOR marker and join to work in the round.

Ribbing Round: (P2, k1) rep to end.

Work the Ribbing Round until your work measures 1.25 inches (3 cm).

Cowl Body

Change to LARGER needles and join MC.

Round 1: Using MC, (k11, sl1p wyib) 10 times.

Round 2: Using CC, (k5, sl1p wyib, k6) 10 times.

Rep Rounds 1 and 2 until the cowl measures 16 inches (40 cm) from the CO edge. Work Round 1 once more.

Break MC, leaving a 6-inch (15-cm) tail.

Lower Hem

You will continue to work in CC only. Change to SMALLER needles.

Ribbing Round: (P2, k1) rep to end.

Work the Ribbing Round until the ribbing measures 1.25 inches (3 cm).

You will now split for the front and back ribbing. You will be binding off 4 sts total. Binding off these sts will leave a st on your RH needle. Leave this stitch on your RH needle, then continue to work in pattern.

Division Round: BO 2 sts, (p2, k1) 19 times, BO 2 sts, (p2, k1) 19 times.

Place the next 58 sts on a piece of scrap yarn.

You should now have 58 sts on your needles. These are your Front Hem sts. You have 58 sts on a piece of scrap yarn. These are you Back Hem sts.

Front Hem

You will no longer be working in the round. You will begin with a WS row.

Next Row (WS): Sl1p wyif, (k2, p1) 19 times.

Row 1 (RS): Sl1k wyib, (p2, k1) 19 times.

Row 2 (WS): Sl1p wyif, (k2, p1) 19 times.

Rep Rows 1 and 2 until the Front Hem measures 4 inches (10 cm).

BO all sts in pattern. Break CC, leaving a 6-inch (15-cm) tail.

Back Hem

Place the 58 held sts back on your SMALLER needles.

Beginning on a RS row, rep the Front Hem section until the Back Hem is the same length as the Front Hem. BO all sts in pattern. Break CC, leaving a 6-inch (15-cm) tail.

Finishing

Weave in all ends. For the best results, be sure to wet block your finished cowl. Soak the cowl in cold water, squeezing to remove air bubbles. Squeeze out the water, but do not wring. Roll the cowl in a dry towel, burrito-style, and press on it to remove excess water. Lay the cowl flat to dry, using a measuring tape to be sure it is laid out with the correct dimensions.

Rainbow Blowout Cowl

Skill Level: Adventurous Beginner

At the end of practically every project, I have just a little bit of yarn leftover. The leftovers get thrown into a tub or fall to the bottom of my knitting bag. The Rainbow Blowout Cowl is the perfect project to bring all of your leftover bits and bobs together. Leave this project on your needles and add to it every time you have a pretty little yarn remnant. This cowl includes five distinct stitch motifs that all look great when working in self-striping yarn. I have provided specific instructions for a cowl just like mine, but you can use this pattern as a formula for your own fun cowl. Feel free to mix these sections up. Make them shorter or longer to fit your yarn and yardage. Add length to your cowl or shorten it. Get the most out of your scraps of self-striping yarn and just have fun!

Construction

This cowl begins with a Provisional cast on (see page 178). Then the cowl is knit in the round. Once you have knit your desired length, the live sts from the end of the cowl are joined to the sts from the Provisional cast on using the Kitchener Stitch method (see page 181).

Maximum Stitches Used for a Self-Striping Round: 77

Sizes

One Size (adjustable length)

See the Finished Measurements on page 92.

Yarn

- Fingering weight yarn, Turtlepurl Striped Turtle Toes
- (100% superwash merino, 220 yards / 3.5 ounces [201 m / 100 g])
- Samples shown in "Save a Horse," "Derby," "Twilight," "City Girl," "Bruised," "Crushed," "Tickled Pink," "The Artist B-Sides" and "Diamond Dungarees"
- 9 mini skeins
- 500 yards (457 m)

Yarn Notes

I used nine mini skeins to knit this cowl. Each mini skein was distinct and didn't technically "match" any other mini. If you have your own mini skeins or leftovers, don't spend too much time worrying about matching up your colors. Throw all your minis in a bag and choose the next color at random.

Needles

Two sets of US 3 (3.25 mm) 16-inch (40-cm) circular needles, or as required to meet gauge

Gauge

24 stitches and 28 rounds = 4 inches (10 cm) in stockinette stitch after blocking

Notions

- 1 stitch marker
- Scissors
- Scrap yarn
- Tapestry needle
- Tape measure

Finished Measurements
A. **Circumference:** 44 inches (110 cm)
B. **Width:** 12.75 inches (32 cm)

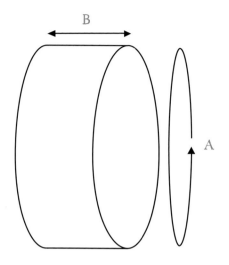

Abbreviations

BOR	beginning of round
CO	cast on
dec	decrease
inc	increase
k	knit
k2tog	knit two together
m	marker
LT	left twist
m1L	make one left
m1R	make one right
p	purl
rep	repeat
RT	right twist
sl1p	slip one purlwise
ssk	slip, slip, knit
st(s)	stitch(es)
wyib	with yarn in back

Pattern

Note: I have not provided instructions for when to join a new color of yarn in this pattern. For my minis, I knit each mini skein until I had just enough yarn left to weave in an end. I joined new colors in the middle of rounds so that I could use every last bit of my mini skeins.

Using a Provisional cast on, CO 77 sts. Place a BOR marker and join to work in the round.

Note: If the Provisional cast on method is new to you, see page 178 for more information on how to work this cast on.

Section One: Dip Stitches

Knit four rounds.

Round 1: (K4, Dip Left, k3, Dip Right) 11 times. [22 sts inc; 99 total sts]

Round 2: (K4, sl1p wyib, k3, sl1p wyib) 11 times.

Round 3: (K4, ssk, k1, k2tog) 11 times. [22 sts dec; 77 total sts]

Round 4-8: K all.

Rep Rounds 1–8 an additional six times.

Note: See page 184 for more information on how to work the Dip Left and Dip Right techniques.

Section Two: Twisted Stitches

Round 1: (K5, RT) 11 times.

Round 2: (K4, RT, k1) 11 times.

Round 3: (K3, RT, k2) 11 times.

Round 4: (K2, RT, k3) 11 times.

Round 5: (K1, RT, k4) 11 times.

Round 6: (RT, k5) 11 times.

Round 7: (K1, LT, k4) 11 times.

Round 8: (K2, LT, k3) 11 times.

Round 9: (K3, LT, k2) 11 times.

Round 10: (K4, LT, k1) 11 times.

Rep Rounds 1–10 an additional five times.

Knit five rounds.

Note: See page 184 for more information on how to work Left Twist and Right Twist sts.

Section Three: Feather & Fan

Round 1: P all.

Round 2: Sl1p wyib, k to end.

Round 3: [Ssk twice, (m1R, k1) 2 times, m1L, k1, m1L, k2tog twice] 7 times.

Round 4 and 5: K all.

Rep Rounds 1–5 an additional eleven times.

Section Four: Slipped Stitches

Round 1-4: (Sl1p wyib, k6) 11 times.

Round 5: K all.

Rep Rounds 1–5 an additional eleven times.

Knit four rounds.

Section Five: Knits & Purls

Round 1-4: (K4, p3) 11 times.

Round 5-8: (P3, k4) 11 times.

Rep Rounds 1–8 an additional six times.

Knit four rounds.

Joining the Ends

Remove the scrap yarn from your Provisional cast on and place these CO sts onto a second set of needles. With a tapestry needle, use the Kitchener Stitch method (see page 181) to graft the two ends of your cowl together. Be careful not to twist your work.

Finishing

Weave in all ends. For the best results, be sure to wet block your finished cowl. Soak the cowl in cold water, squeezing to remove air bubbles. Squeeze out the water, but do not wring. Roll the cowl in a dry towel, burrito-style, and press on it to remove excess water. Lay the cowl flat to dry, using a measuring tape to be sure it is laid out with the correct dimensions.

Radiant Rainbow

Shawls That Thrill

I have a secret. It's a doozy, so make sure you keep it to yourself. Definitely don't tell the mittens or the hats. No telling. Got it? Great.

SELF-STRIPING SHAWLS ARE COMPLETELY AND TOTALLY AH-MAZING! Phew. I've been dying for you to get to this page. I can hardly wait to share these shawls with you. Unlike the smaller projects in the previous chapters, though I love mittens deeply, the projects in this chapter are big, thrilling showstoppers.

The shawls in this chapter are designed to stop strangers in their tracks. These projects take everything you've learned so far and amp it up: bigger shapes, longer stretches of self-striping yarn, endless color combinations, but with the same easy-to-knit stitches and fun techniques. Do you remember how the short rows changed your stripes in the Leapfrog Mittens (page 33)? Wait until you see what you can do with short rows in the Onward & Outward Shawl (page 109). Did you enjoy combining two colors last chapter in the Encompassing Cowl (page 87)? How about taking it up a notch in the three-color Daring Double Shawl (page 115)? You've been honing your rainbow skills, but now is your chance to really show off.

Seriously though, don't tell the mittens. Every time one of the mittens gets upset, it goes missing, and I have to knit another one.

Indicator Shawl

Skill Level: Beginner

Sometimes it is just hard to start small. Hats are lovely, and everyone loves mittens, but even beginners want projects that WOW! This beginner pattern is all about learning basic techniques for knitting with self-striping yarn while getting BIG results. Using increases and decreases, you will make a beautiful arrow-shaped wrap or scarf that bends the stripes in your self-striping yarn. Packed with tips and tricks, this pattern will help you make tidy transitions between stripes using two of the most common stitches for a new knitter: garter and stockinette stitch. Although this pattern was written to help knitters who are new to self-striping yarn, the Indicator Shawl is a relaxing, satisfying knit for all levels.

Construction

The Indicator is cast on at the V-shaped end and worked until you reach your target length. It is then bound off at the pointed end of the scarf or wrap (whichever you choose to knit). This pattern includes instructions for working either a scarf or a wrap.

Maximum Stitches Used for a Self-Striping Row: 61 (125)

Sizes

Scarf (Wrap)

See the Finished Measurements on page 98.

Yarn

- Fingering weight yarn, Gauge Dyeworks Sweater
- (80% superwash merino and 20% nylon, 655 yards / 6 ounces [599 m / 170 g])
- Sample shown in "White Light + Dark Blue"
- 1 (2) skeins
- 655 (1310) yards / [599 (1198) m]

Yarn Notes

This pattern was knit using an unusual self-striping yarn that was originally created for a baby sweater. I love the long sections of solid blue in this yarn, bordered on either end by a rainbow and a stretch of green. Feel free to substitute self-striping yarn with regular color changes or combine a self-striping yarn with a solid main color. This is a great project for experimentation!

Needles

US 7 (4.5 mm) 32-inch (80-cm) circular needles, or as required to meet gauge

Gauge

18 stitches and 26 rows = 4 inches (10 cm) in stockinette stitch after blocking

Notions

- 3 stitch markers
- Scissors
- Tapestry needle
- Tape measure

Finished Measurements

Sample is shown in the Wrap size.

NOTE: The length measurement for your scarf or wrap will vary based on your combination of lace, stockinette and garter stitch. If you achieve stitch gauge, then the depth of your wrap will be consistent with the measurement below. Gauge is not critical for this pattern. However, changes in gauge will result in changes in yardage and finished dimensions.

A. **Length:** 75 (75) inches / [188 (188) cm]

B. **Depth:** 11.5 (23.5) inches / [29 (59) cm]

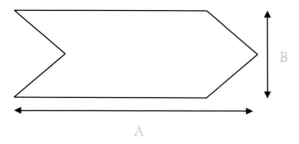

Abbreviations

BO	bind off
CO	cast on
cdd	central double decrease
k	knit
m	marker
p	purl
pm	place marker
rep	repeat
rm	remove marker
RS	right side
sl1p	slip one purlwise
sm	slip marker
st(s)	stitch(es)
WS	wrong side
wyif	with yarn in front
yo	yarn over

Pattern

This pattern gives you the chance to play with the stripes in your yarn and create simple textures by using garter stitches and stockinette stitches. This is not a traditional pattern. Instead, this is a recipe for creating your own personal Indicator wrap or scarf.

Note on Gauge: I have provided the plain stockinette gauge for this pattern, because it is the easiest st to swatch in preparation for your wrap or scarf. However, you will find that the increases and decreases that create the arrow shape in this pattern warp the stockinette. This is why the depth measurement is smaller than you would expect based on the number of sts you cast on.

Use the following steps to create your own Indicator:

Step 1: CO 61 (125) sts.

Step 2: Work the Set-Up Section.

Step 3: Work at least 1 inch (2.5 cm) of the Garter Section in order to prevent curling along the CO edge.

Step 4: Work any combination of the Garter Section and Stockinette Section according to your taste. Be sure to read the Creating Clean Transitions section in order to make the tidiest transitions when you have a color change.

Step 5: Finish your Indicator with at least 1 inch (2.5 cm) of the Garter Section to prevent curling at the end of your piece. End after completing a RS row.

Step 6: BO all sts knitwise on a WS row.

Set-Up Section

Row 1 (RS): Sl1p wyif, k2, pm, k29 (61), pm, k26 (58), pm, k3.

Row 2 (WS): Sl1p wyif, k2, sm, k to m, sm, k1, p1, k to m, sm, k3.

> Note: The total number of sts will remain constant throughout the wrap. However, your marker will continue to shift 1 stitch to the left every RS row. After completing each RS row, you should have 3 sts, a border marker, 29 (61) sts, a central marker, 26 (58) sts, a border marker, and 3 sts. This will be a total of 61 (125) sts.

Garter Section

Row 1 (RS): Sl1p wyif, k2, sm, yo, k to 3 sts before m, cdd, rm, k1, pm, k to m, yo, sm, k3.

Row 2 (WS): Sl1p wyif, k2, sm, k to m, sm, k1, p1, k to m, sm, k3.

Rep Garter Rows 1 and 2 until you reach your desired length or a color change in your yarn. End after completing a WS row.

Stockinette Section

Row 1 (RS): Sl1p wyif, k2, sm, yo, k to 3 sts before m, cdd, rm, k1, pm, k to m, yo, sm, k3.

Row 2 (WS): Sl1p wyif, k2, sm, (p to m, sm) 2 times, k3.

Rep Stockinette Rows 1 and 2 until you reach your desired length or a color change in your yarn. End after completing a WS row.

Creating Clean Transitions

Changing between garter and stockinette at the same time that your yarn changes color is a great way to make your stripes really pop. However, working with different textures and dealing with color transitions can create new challenges.

The Indicator pattern was written to help you deal with the most common issue when working with self-striping yarn and knitting flat: When you reach a new color, you will almost certainly be in the middle of a row. Sometimes this will occur on a RS row, and sometimes this will occur on a WS row. Here are a few tips on how to make these transitions look beautiful and tidy:

How to change from stockinette to garter stitch when there is a color change on a RS row:

Complete the RS row according to Row 1 of the Garter Section. On the next (WS) row, begin working according to Row 2 of the Garter Section. When you reach the color transition, complete the row according to Stockinette Row 2. On the next (RS) row, continue to work according to the Garter Section instructions until you are ready to make another transition.

How to change from stockinette to garter stitch when there is a color change on a WS row:

Complete the WS row according to Stockinette Section Row 2. On the next (RS) row, begin working according to the Garter Section instructions and continue until you are ready to make another transition.

Finishing

Weave in all ends. For the best results, be sure to wet block your finished Indicator. Soak the shawl in cold water, squeezing to remove air bubbles. Squeeze out the water, but do not wring. Roll the shawl in a dry towel, burrito-style, and press on it to remove excess water. Lay the shawl flat to dry, using a measuring tape to be sure it is laid out with the correct dimensions.

How to transition from garter to stockinette stitch when there is a color change on a RS row:

Complete the RS row according to Row 1 of the Garter Section. On the next (WS) row, begin working according to Row 2 of the Stockinette Section. On the next (RS) row, continue to work according to the Stockinette Section instructions until you are ready to make another transition.

How to transition from garter to stockinette stitch when there is a color change on a WS row:

Work to the color change according to Garter Section Row 2. When you reach the color change, begin working according to Row 2 (WS) of the Stockinette Section. On the next (RS) row, continue to work according to the Stockinette Section instructions until you are ready to make another transition.

For the Thrill Shawl

Skill Level: Intermediate

When I wound this self-striping yarn, I practically fell out of my chair. To my delight, there were twenty beautiful stripes of rainbow goodness in each color repeat! As a longtime lover of yarn, it was exhilarating! The For the Thrill Shawl was designed to celebrate each beautiful stripe in this yarn without leaving a single color out. Combining short rows and attached edgings, this shawl is a thrilling knit from top to bottom. You will turn your stripes on their side, rock garter stitch wedges and knit airy eyelets to create this playful crescent-shaped shawl. Best of all, your self-striping yarn will have the chance to really shine in the long stretches of vertical stripes.

Construction

This shawl is knit from the top down. It begins with a Garter Tab cast on and a small crescent. Then stitches are cast on and an attached lace border is worked vertically. After working the attached border, a garter wedge is worked using the Wrap & Turn Short Rows method (see page 184). After working a second attached lace edging and a second garter wedge, the shawl is completed with an eyelet lace border.

Maximum Stitches Used for a Self-Striping Row: 103

Sizes

One Size

See the Finished Measurements on page 103.

Yarn

- Fingering weight yarn, Kirby Wirby Soft & Squishy
- (75% superwash merino and 25% nylon, 440 yards / 3.5 ounces [402 m / 100 g])
- Fingering weight yarn, Leading Men Fiber Arts Show Stopper
- (75% merino and 25% nylon, 463 yards / 3.5 ounces [423 m / 100 g]), CC1
- Fingering weight yarn, Lemonade Shop Mighty Sock
- (75% superwash merino and 25% nylon, 463 yards / 3.5 ounces [423 m / 100 g]), CC2
- 1 skein of MC, 1 skein of CC1 and 1 skein of CC2
- Sample shown in "Hells to the Yes!" (MC, self-striping), "My Lipstick Be Poppin" (CC1, pink) and "Hippo Disco" (CC2, gray speckle)
- **Main Color:** 290 yards (265 m)
- **Contrasting Color 1:** 215 yards (197 m)
- **Contrasting Color 2:** 330 yards (302 m)

Yarn Notes

This pattern was knit using a four-ply fingering weight yarn. I combined a self-striping, solid and speckled yarn for this shawl. Using the colors in the self-striping, I chose colors that would highlight my favorite colors in the self-striping yarn without distracting from its beauty. All three yarns have the same fiber content, and together they make a mighty, thrilling knit!

Needles

US 5 (3.75 mm) 32-inch (80-cm) circular needles, or as required to meet gauge

Gauge

22 stitches and 36 rows = 4 inches (10 cm) in garter stitch after blocking

Notions

- 2 stitch markers
- Scissors
- Tapestry needle
- Blocking wires or pins
- Tape measure

Finished Measurements

A. **Length:** 61 inches (152.5 cm)

B. **Depth:** 22 inches (55 cm)

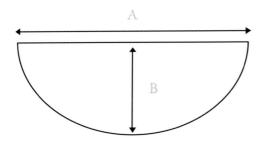

Abbreviations	
BO	bind off
CC	contrasting color
CO	cast on
dec	decrease
inc	increase
k	knit
k2tog	knit two together
LH	left-hand
MC	main color
p	purl
pm	place marker
rep	repeat
rm	remove marker
RS	right side
sl1k	slip one knitwise
sl1p	slip one purlwise
sm	slip marker
ssk	slip, slip, knit
st(s)	stitch(es)
WS	wrong side
wyib	with yarn in back
wyif	with yarn in front
w&t	wrap and turn
yo	yarn over

Pattern

Section 1: Striped Crescent

Garter Tab Cast On: Using MC, CO 3 sts, knit nine rows, turn work 90 degrees clockwise, then pick up and knit 4 sts along the left edge (one in each garter ridge). Turn work 90 degrees, then pick up 3 sts along the CO edge. [10 sts]

Set-Up Row (WS): Sl1p wyif, k2, pm, p4, pm, k3.

Row 1 (RS): Sl1p wyif, k2, sm, (yo, k1) 4 times, yo, sm, k3. [5 sts inc; 15 sts total]

Row 2 (WS): Sl1p wyif, k2, sm, p to m, sm, k3.

Row 3 (RS): Sl1p wyif, k2, sm, k to m, sm, k3.

Row 4 (WS): Sl1p wyif, k2, sm, p to m, sm, k3.

Row 5 (RS): Sl1p wyif, k2, sm, (yo, k1) 9 times, yo, sm, k3. [10 sts inc; 25 sts total]

Row 6 (WS): Sl1p wyif, k2, sm, p to m, sm, k3.

Row 7 (RS): Sl1p wyif, k2, sm, k to m, sm, k3.

Row 8 (WS): Sl1p wyif, k2, sm, p to m, sm, k3.

Row 9 (RS): Sl1p wyif, k2, sm, (yo, k2tog) 9 times, yo, k1, yo, sm, k3. [2 sts inc; 27 sts total]

Row 10 (WS): Sl1p wyif, k2, sm, p to m, sm, k3.

Row 11 (RS): Sl1p wyif, k2, sm, k to m, sm, k3.

Row 12 (WS): Sl1p wyif, k2, sm, p to m, sm, k3.

Row 13 (RS): Sl1p wyif, k2, sm, (yo, k1) 21 times, yo, sm, k3. [22 sts inc; 49 sts total]

Rep Rows 10–12.

Row 17 (RS): Sl1p wyif, k2, sm, (yo, k2tog) 21 times, yo, k1, yo, sm, k3. [2 sts inc; 51 sts total]

Rep Rows 10–12.

Row 21 (RS): Sl1p wyif, k2, sm, (yo, k2tog) 22 times, yo, k1, yo, sm, k3. [2 sts inc; 53 sts total]

Rep Rows 10–12.

Row 25 (RS): Sl1p wyif, k2, sm, (yo, k1) 47 times, yo, sm, k3. [48 sts inc; 101 sts total]

Rep Rows 10–12.

Row 29 (RS): Sl1p wyif, k2, sm, (yo, k2tog) 47 times, yo, k1, yo, sm, k3. [2 sts inc; 103 sts total]

Row 30 (WS): Sl1p wyif, k2, rm, p to m, rm, k3.

Section 2: First Rainbow Border

With the RS facing you, as you continue to work with your MC, use the Cable cast on method to cast 25 sts onto your LH needle (in front of the sts worked in Row 30 of Section 1). You will now have 128 sts on your needles (25 new border sts and the original 103 crescent sts).

Row 1 (RS): Sl1k wyib, k20, p1, sl1p wyib, p1, ssk (1 st from the border with 1 st from the crescent), turn work. [1 st dec]

Row 2 (WS): Sl1p wyif, k1, p1, k to end.

Row 3 (RS): Sl1k wyib, k20, p1, sl1p wyib, p1, ssk (1 st from the border with 1 st from the crescent), turn work. [1 st dec]

Row 4 (WS): Sl1p wyif, k1, p1, k to end.

Row 5 (RS): Sl1k wyib, (k2tog, yo) 10 times, p1, sl1p wyib, p1, ssk (1 st from the border with 1 st from the crescent), turn work. [1 st dec]

Row 6 (WS): Sl1p wyif, k1, p1, k1, p to end.

Row 7 (RS): Sl1k wyib, k20, p1, sl1p wyib, p1, ssk (1 st from the border with 1 st from the crescent), turn work. [1 st dec]

Row 8 (WS): Sl1p wyif, k1, p1, k1, p to end.

Rep Rows 5–8 until you have a total of 28 sts on your needles (25 border sts and 3 crescent sts). Work Row 5 once more.

Next Row (WS): Sl1p wyif, k1, p1, k to end.

Next Row (RS): Sl1k wyib, k20, p1, sl1p wyib, p1, ssk (1 st from the border with 1 st from the crescent), turn work. [1 st dec]

Next Row (WS): Sl1p wyif, k1, p1, k to end.

Next Row (RS): Sl1k wyib, k20, p1, sl1p wyib, p1, ssk (1 st from the border with 1 st from the crescent), turn work. [1 st dec]

Next Row (WS): BO all sts knitwise. Break MC, leaving a 6-inch (15-cm) tail.

Section 3: First Short Row Wedge

With the RS facing you, using CC1, pick up and knit 103 sts along the slipped st edge of the First Rainbow Border. You will be picking up one st for each slipped st along the First Rainbow Border.

Next Row (WS): Sl1p wyif, k2, pm, k to last 3 sts, pm, k3.

Row 1 (RS): Sl1p wyif, k2, sm, (yo, k1) rep to m, yo, sm, k3. [98 sts inc; 201 sts total]

Row 2 (WS): Sl1p wyif, k2, sm, k to m, sm, k3.

Join CC2. Do not break CC1.

You will now begin working in short rows.

Note: See page 184 for information on how to work Wrap & Turn Short Rows.

Row 3 (RS): Sl1p wyif, k2, sm, k to m, sm, k3.

Row 4 (WS): Sl1p wyif, k2, sm, k to last 5 sts, w&t.

Row 5 (RS): K to m, sm, k3.

Row 6 (WS): Sl1p wyif, k2, sm, k to 15 sts before last wrapped st, w&t.

Row 7 (RS): K to m, sm, k3.

Rep Rows 6 and 7 an additional eleven times.

Note: When working in garter stitch, there is no need to pick up and knit the wraps of wrapped stitches. Simply knit these stitches normally.

Row 30 (WS): Sl1p wyif, k2, sm, k to m, sm, k2, sl1p wyif.

Change to CC1. Do not break CC2.

Row 31 (RS): Sl1p wyif, k2, sm, k to m, sm, k3.

Row 32 (WS): Sl1p wyif, k2, sm, k to m, sm, k3.

Row 33 (RS): Sl1p wyif, k2, sm, (yo, k2tog) rep to 1 st before m, yo, k1, yo, sm, k3. [2 sts inc; 203 sts total]

Row 34 (WS): Sl1p wyif, k2, sm, k to m, sm, k3.

Change to CC2. Do not break CC1.

Work Rows 3–34 once more [205 sts]. When you repeat Row 34, remove markers as you come to them.

The following row is a set-up row for Section 4.

Next Row (RS): Using CC1, sl1p wyif, k to end.

Break CC1 and CC2, leaving a 6-inch (15-cm) tail.

Section 4: Second Rainbow Border

With the RS facing you, join MC and, using the Cable cast on method, CO 21 sts to your LH needle (in front of the last row of Section 3 sts). You will now have 226 sts on your needles (21 new border sts and the original 205 crescent sts).

Next Row (WS): Sl1p wyif, k1, p1, k to end.

Next Row (RS): Sl1k wyib, k16, p1, sl1p wyib, p1, ssk (1 st from the border with 1 st from the crescent), turn work. [1 st dec]

Next Row (WS): Sl1p wyif, k1, p1, k to end.

Next Row (RS): Sl1k wyib, k16, p1, sl1p wyib, p1, ssk (1 st from the border with 1 st from the crescent), turn work. [1 st dec]

Next Row (WS): BO all sts knitwise. Break MC, leaving a 6-inch (15-cm) tail.

Section 5: Second Short Row Wedge

With the RS facing you, using CC1, pick up and knit 205 sts along the slipped st edge of the Second Rainbow Border. You will be picking up one st for each slipped st along the Second Rainbow Border.

Next Row (WS): Sl1p wyif, k2, pm, k to last 3 sts, pm, k3.

Row 1 (RS): Sl1p wyif, k2, sm, (yo, k2tog) rep to 1 st before m, yo, k1, yo, sm, k3. [2 sts inc; 207 sts total]

Row 2 (WS): Sl1p wyif, k2, sm, k to m, sm, k3.

Join CC2. Break CC1, leaving a 6-inch (15-cm) tail. You will now begin working in short rows.

Row 3 (RS): Sl1p wyif, k2, sm, k to m, sm, k2, sl1p wyif.

Row 4 (WS): Sl1p wyif, k2, sm, k to m, sm, k3.

Row 5 (RS): Sl1p wyif, k2, sm, k to last 5 sts, w&t.

Row 6 (WS): K to m, sm, k3.

Row 7 (RS): Sl1p wyif, k2, sm, k to 15 sts before last wrapped st, w&t.

Row 8 (WS): K to m, sm, k3.

Rep Rows 7 and 8 an additional eleven times.

Join CC1. Break CC2, leaving a 6-inch (15-cm) tail.

Row 1 (RS): Sl1k wyib, k16, p1, sl1p wyib, p1, ssk (1 st from the border with 1 st from the crescent), turn work. [1 st dec]

Row 2 (WS): Sl1p wyif, k1, p1, k to end.

Row 3 (RS): Sl1k wyib, k16, p1, sl1p wyib, p1, ssk (1 st from the border with 1 st from the crescent), turn work. [1 st dec]

Row 4 (WS): Sl1p wyif, k1, p1, k to end.

Row 5 (RS): Sl1k wyib, (k2tog, yo) 8 times, p1, sl1p wyib, p1, ssk (1 st from the border with 1 st from the crescent), turn work. [1 st dec]

Row 6 (WS): Sl1p wyif, k1, p1, k1, p to end.

Row 7 (RS): Sl1k wyib, k16, p1, sl1p wyib, p1, ssk (1 st from the border with 1 st from the crescent), turn work. [1 st dec]

Row 8 (WS): Sl1p wyif, k1, p1, k1, p to end.

Rep Rows 5–8 until you have a total of 24 sts on your needles (21 border sts and 3 crescent sts). Work Row 5 once more.

Row 31 (RS): Sl1p wyif, k2, sm, k to m, sm, k3.

Row 32 (WS): Sl1p wyif, k2, sm, k to m, sm, k3.

Row 33 (RS): Sl1p wyif, k2, sm, (yo, k2tog) rep to 1 st before m, yo, k1, yo, sm, k3. [2 sts inc; 209 sts total]

Row 34 (WS): Sl1p wyif, k2, sm, k to m, sm, k3.

You should now have 209 sts on your needles. Break CC1, leaving a 6-inch (15-cm) tail.

Join CC2 and work Rows 3–34 once more. You should now have 211 sts on your needles.

Section 6: Eyelet Border

Change to CC2.

> Note: When working the Eyelet Border, do not break the yarn with each color change. Carry the color that is not being used on the backside of your work.

Row 1 (RS): Sl1p wyif, k2, sm, k to m, sm, k3.

Row 2 (WS): Sl1p wyif, k2, sm, k to m, sm, k3.

Row 3 (RS): Sl1p wyif, k2, sm, (yo, k2tog) rep to 1 st before m, yo, k1, yo, sm, k3. [2 sts inc]

Row 4 (WS): Sl1p wyif, k2, sm, k to m, sm, k3.

Work Rows 1–4 in CC2 (213 sts). Change to CC1. Work Rows 1–4, alternating CC1 and CC2 until you have worked Rows 1–4 a total of four times. End with CC1 on a WS row. You should now have 219 sts on your needles.

Break CC2, leaving a 6-inch (15-cm) tail.

Picot Bind Off (RS): With CC1, (CO 2, BO 4, move last BO st from RH needle back to LH needle) rep to last 3 sts, CO 2, BO 5.

> Note: When working the Picot Bind Off, there are several different CO and BO sts you can use. However, I recommend using the Cable cast on method (see page 177) and a standard BO.

Break CC1, leaving a 6-inch (15-cm) tail.

Finishing

Weave in all ends. For the best results, be sure to wet block your finished shawl. Soak the shawl in cold water, squeezing to remove air bubbles. Squeeze out the water, but do not wring. Roll the shawl in a dry towel, burrito-style, and press on it to remove excess water. Lay the shawl flat to dry, using a measuring tape to be sure it is laid out with the correct dimensions. Use blocking pins or wires to open up the simple lace in this dramatic shawl, as follows:

Beginning at the top center, use blocking wires or blocking pins to create a straight upper edge. If you are using blocking pins, place a pin at the top center and then work back and forth, placing a pin to the right of center, then left of center, then right of the rightmost pin, then left of the leftmost pin, and so on, until you reach the end of the upper edge. Do not worry if your upper edge is not perfectly straight; do your best. Use your measuring tape to be sure that the shawl is laid out with the correct dimensions.

After the upper edge is blocked in place, begin pinning the lower edge. Begin at the center and work outward in the same manner as the upper edge. You can also use flexible blocking wires to create the same effect by threading the wire through the point of each eyelet hole.

> Note: You may find that you need to adjust the placement of the pins along the upper edge of the shawl as you pin the lower edge.

Onward & Outward Shawl

Skill Level: Intermediate

When I was a kid, my sister had an incredible knack for finding the perfect skipping stones. We would spend hours at the creek filling our pockets with rocks, then making them hop across the water. The self-striping yarn at the center of this shawl reminds me of a skipping stone, whizzing across the top of the water, causing ripples in the creek's surface. The Onward & Outward Shawl was designed for fun. The unusual construction in this shawl gives you the chance to play with your yarn as you create short row wedges that warp and stretch the stripes. The dramatic result is surprisingly simple and extremely fun to knit!

Construction

This shawl is knit from the center out. The shawl begins with eight equal wedges, knit flat using German Short Rows (see page 184) to create a circle. Then, an eyelet border is picked up and worked in the round. Finally, a portion of the stitches are bound off and each end of the shawl is knit flat.

Maximum Stitches Used for a Self-Striping Row: 50

Sizes

One Size

See the Finished Measurements on page 110.

Yarn

- Fingering weight yarn, Knitterly Things Vesper Sock
- (80% superwash merino and 20% nylon, 430 yards / 3.5 ounces [393 m / 100 g])
- Sample shown in "Brilliantly Bold" (MC, self-striping), "Deep Teal" (CC1, blue) and "Deep Orchid" (CC2, purple)
- 1 skein of MC, 1 skein of CC1 and 1 skein of CC2
- **Main Color:** 350 yards (320 m)
- **Contrasting Color 1:** 430 yards (393 m)
- **Contrasting Color 2:** 430 yards (393 m)

Yarn Notes

This shawl was knit using a bright, graphic self-striping yarn. I chose two coordinating colors that would complement, but not overpower, the self-striping yarn so that those beautiful stripes would be the center of attention.

Needles

US 7 (4.5 mm) 32-inch (80-cm) circular needles, or as required to meet gauge

A DPN or other needle in the same size for three-needle bind off

Gauge

20 stitches and 26 rows = 4 inches (10 cm) in stockinette stitch after blocking

Notions

- 4 stitch markers
- 1 stitch marker
- Scissors
- Tapestry needle
- Tape measure

Finished Measurements

A. **Length:** 64 inches (160 cm)

B. **Depth:** 23 inches (57.5 cm)

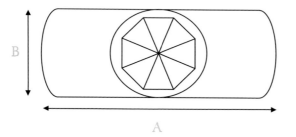

Abbreviations	
BO	bind off
BOR	beginning of round
CC	contrasting color
CO	cast on
dec	decrease
DS	double stitch
inc	increase
k	knit
k2tog	knit two together
m	marker
MC	main color
p	purl
pm	place marker
rep	repeat
RH	right-hand
RS	right side
sl1k	slip one knitwise
sl1p	slip one purlwise
sm	slip marker
ssk	slip, slip, knit
st(s)	stitch(es)
WS	wrong side
wyib	with yarn in back
wyif	with yarn in front
yo	yarn over

Pattern

Using MC, CO 50 sts.

Central Wedges

Set-Up Row (WS): Sl1p wyif, p to end.

Row 1 (RS): Sl1k wyib, k to end.

Row 2 (WS): Sl1p wyif, p to last st, turn work.

Row 3 (RS): DS, k to end.

Row 4 (WS): Sl1p wyif, p to 1 st before last DS, turn work.

Rep Rows 3 and 4 an additional 22 times. Rep Row 3 once more. On a RS row, this will leave 2 sts between the beginning of the row and the final DS.

With the RS facing you, slide your work from one end of your circular knitting needle to the other end. You are now ready to work a RS row at the small end of your wedge.

Join CC1.

Row 5 (RS): K, resolving all DS sts as you come to them.

Row 6 (WS): K all.

With the WS facing you, slide your work from one end of your circular knitting needle to the other end. You are now ready to work a WS row at the large end of your wedge. Change to MC.

Beginning with the Set-Up Row, rep the entire Central Wedge section an additional seven times. Each time you begin a new Central Wedge section, you will use the MC. Do not break MC or CC1 while working the individual wedges. When you work the final wedge (Wedge 8), end after completing Row 5 (RS). Break MC and CC1, leaving a 6-inch (15-cm) tail for each color. Leave sts on your needles.

> **Note:** If you are trying to create identical wedges, you may need to break the MC at the end of each wedge section. In order to create identical wedges, begin each wedge with the same color in your self-striping sequence.

Joining the Wedges

Using CC1 and with the RS facing you, pick up and knit 50 sts along the CO edge of the first wedge. Align the live sts from Wedge 8 with the picked up sts from Wedge 1. Place the WS of the wedges together. Using a third needle, BO all sts using the three-needle bind off (see page 180). The BO will create an exposed seam that mimics a garter ridge on the RS of your work. Break CC1, leaving a 6-inch (15-cm) tail.

Closing the Hole

When you have joined the wedges, you will find that there is a hole at the center of your work. To close this hole, place one of the tails of CC1 near the center of your work on a tapestry needle. Insert the tapestry needle into the first CC1 purl bump at the base of each wedge around the opening of the hole (Photos 1 and 2). Insert the tapestry needle back into the first purl bump (Photo 3). Insert the tapestry needle through the center of the hole from RS to WS. Pull the yarn snuggly to tighten the hole closed. Weave in the tail on the WS of your work.

Wedge Border

Begin at a garter ridge where two wedges meet. With the RS facing you, using CC1, pick up and knit 208 sts around the outer edge of your wedge circle. You will be picking up 26 sts along the edge of each wedge. Place a BOR marker and join to work in the round.

Round 1: P all.

Round 2: (Yo, k2) rep to end. [104 sts inc; 312 sts total]

Round 3: P all.

Round 4: K all.

Round 5: P all.

Round 6: (Yo, k2tog) rep to end.

Round 7: P all.

Round 8: K all.

Round 9: P all.

Rep Rounds 6-9 once more.

In the following row, you will divide your sts into two equal sections. To do this, you will BO two sets of sts. Binding off these sts will leave a st on your RH needle. Leave this st on your RH needle and continue to work in pattern as instructed.

Set-Up Round: [BO 39, k2, (yo, ssk) 3 times, k30, pm, k39, pm, k30, (k2tog, yo) 3 times, k3] 2 times.

You should now have two sets of 117 sts on your needles. Place the first set of 117 sts on a piece of scrap yarn. These are your Left End sts. You will continue to work the Right End sts.

Right End

You will no longer be working in the round. You will work the Right End sts flat. The number of sts in this section will remain constant throughout the section. You should have 117 sts on your needles at the end of each row.

Next Row (WS): Sl1p wyif, k to last st, sl1p wyif.

In the following rows, you will change color every two rows on a RS row. Carry your yarn loosely on the WS of your work as you transition between colors to prevent a tight edge on your shawl.

Join CC2.

Row 1 (RS): Using CC2, k3, ssk, k to m, sm, yo, k to m, yo, sm, k to last 5 sts, k2tog, k3.

Row 2 (WS): Using CC2, sl1p wyif, k10, (p to m, sm) 2 times, p to last 11 sts, k10, sl1p wyif.

Change to CC1.

Row 3 (RS): Using CC1, k3, (yo, ssk) 3 times, ssk, k to m, sm, yo, k to m, yo, sm, k to last 11 sts, k2tog, (k2tog, yo) 3 times, k3.

Row 4 (WS): Using CC1, sl1p wyif, k to last st, sl1p wyif.

Rep rows 1-4 an additional thirteen times. Your removable stitch markers should be 11 sts from the beginning and end of the row. Remove each marker and place them in their original positions. You should have a st marker between sts 39 and 40 and a st marker between sts 78 and 79.

In the following rows, you will work four rows in CC2 and two rows in CC1. Remember to carry your yarn loosely on the WS of your work as you transition between colors to prevent a tight edge on your shawl.

Change to CC2.

Row 5 (RS): Using CC2, k3, ssk, k to m, sm, yo, k to m, yo, sm, k to last 5 sts, k2tog, k3.

Row 6 (WS): Using CC2, sl1p wyif, k10, (p to m, sm) 2 times, p to last 11 sts, k10, sl1p wyif.

Row 7 (RS): Same as Row 5.

Row 8 (WS): Same as Row 6.

Change to CC1.

Row 9 (RS): Using CC1, k3, (yo, ssk) 3 times, ssk, k to m, sm, yo, k to m, yo, sm, k to last 11 sts, k2tog, (k2tog, yo) 3 times, k3.

Row 10 (WS): Using CC1, sl1p wyif, k to last st, sl1p wyif.

Rep rows 5–10 an additional eight times. Your removable stitch markers should be 12 sts from the beginning and end of the row. Remove both stitch markers.

In the following rows, you will work eight rows in CC2 and two rows in CC1. Remember to carry your yarn loosely on the WS of your work as you transition between colors to prevent a tight edge on your shawl.

Change to CC2.

Row 11 (RS): Using CC2, k3, ssk, k to last 5 sts, k2tog, k3. [2 sts dec; 115 sts total]

Row 12 (WS): Using CC2, sl1p wyif, k2, ssk, k7, p to last 12 sts, k7, k2tog, k2, sl1p wyif. [2 sts dec; 113 sts total]

Row 13 (RS): Same as row 11. [2 sts dec; 111 sts total]

Row 14 (WS): Same as row 12. [2 sts dec; 109 sts total]

Row 15 (RS): Same as row 11. [2 sts dec; 107 sts total]

Row 16 (WS): Same as row 12. [2 sts dec; 105 sts total]

Row 17 (RS): Same as row 11. [2 sts dec; 103 sts total]

Row 18 (WS): Same as row 12. [2 sts dec; 101 sts total]

Change to CC1.

Row 19 (RS): Using CC1, k3, (yo, ssk) 3 times, ssk, k to last 11 sts, k2tog, (k2tog, yo) 3 times, k3. [2 sts dec; 99 sts total]

Row 20 (WS): Using CC1, sl1p wyif, k to last st, sl1p wyif.

Rep rows 11–20 once more [81 sts]. Break CC1, leaving a 6-inch (15-cm) tail.

Row 21 (RS): Using CC2, k3, ssk, k to last 5 sts, k2tog, k3. [2 sts dec; 79 sts total]

Row 22 (WS): Using CC2, sl1p wyif, k2, ssk, k to last 5 sts, k2tog, k2, sl1p wyif. [2 sts dec; 77 sts total]

Rep Rows 21 and 22 an additional three times [65 sts]. Rep Row 21 once more [63 sts].

Loosely BO all sts knitwise on a WS row. Break CC2, leaving a 6-inch (15-cm) tail.

Left End

Place the held 117 sts on your needles. Beginning on a WS row, rep the Right End section.

Finishing

Weave in all ends. For the best results, be sure to wet block your finished shawl. Soak the shawl in cold water, squeezing to remove air bubbles. Squeeze out the water, but do not wring. Roll the shawl in a dry towel, burrito-style, and press on it to remove excess water. Lay the shawl flat to dry, using a measuring tape to be sure it is laid out with the correct dimensions.

Daring Double Shawl

Skill Level: Intermediate

There are special skeins of yarn that practically dare you to do something spectacular with them. No little project will do when you have a skein as breathtaking as the rainbow gradient in this project. The Daring Double Shawl is all about drama. The garter and ribbed borders help showcase the self-striping yarn in this shawl so that you can focus on those beautiful stripes. Creating a picture frame effect that draws your eyes to the vertical stripes, the Daring Double Shawl will amplify the beauty of any self-striping yarn you choose to knit. This shawl is made up of two triangles, aligned to create a showstopping parallelogram. Are you short on yardage or time? Knit just one triangle to create a beautiful shawl that takes half the yardage and half the time!

Construction

This shawl is made up of two top-down triangles knit flat. Each triangle is knit separately and identically. At the end of the first triangle, half of the stitches are bound off and the remaining stitches are put on hold. Then, the second triangle is knit. At the end of the second triangle, half of the stitches are bound off. The first triangle is then turned so that the two triangles can be aligned along each set of live sts. Finally, the held stitches from the first triangle are bound off together with the remaining stitches from the second triangle.

Maximum Stitches Used for a Self-Striping Row: 20

Sizes

One Size

See the Finished Measurements on page 116.

Yarn

* Fingering weight yarn, Bad Amy Knits 80/20 Sock
* (80% superwash merino and 20% nylon, 400 yards / 3.5 ounces [365 m / 100g])
* Sample shown in "Silver" (MC, gray), "Uber-violet" (CC1, purple) and "Rainbow Gradient Stripe" (CC2, self-striping)
* 2 skeins of MC, 1 skein of CC1 and 2 (1.7-ounce [50-g]) mini skeins of CC2
* **Main Color:** 800 yards (731 m)
* **Contrasting Color 1:** 325 yards (298 m)
* **Contrasting Color 2:** 400 yards (365 m)

Yarn Notes

This pattern was knit using a two-ply fingering weight yarn with an incredible striping pattern that slowly transitions through a large spectrum of colors. This pattern is perfect for yarns with extremely long color repeats.

Needles

Two sets of US 6 (4 mm) 32-inch (80-cm) circular needles, or as required to meet gauge

Gauge

20 stitches and 36 rows = 4 inches (10 cm) in garter stitch after blocking

20 stitches and 28 rows = 4 inches (10 cm) in stockinette stitch after blocking

Notions

- 4 stitch markers
- Scissors
- Tapestry needle
- Tape measure

Finished Measurements

A. **Length:** 60 inches (152.5 cm)

B. **Depth:** 28 inches (71 cm)

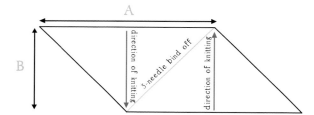

Abbreviations

BO	bind off
CC	contrasting color
CO	cast on
dec	decrease
inc	increase
k	knit
k2tog	knit two together
LH	left-hand
m	marker
MC	main color
p	purl
pm	place marker
rep	repeat
RH	right-hand
rm	remove marker
RS	right side
sl1k	slip one knitwise
sl1p	slip one purlwise
sm	slip marker
ssk	slip, slip, knit
st(s)	stitch(es)
WS	wrong side
w&t	wrap and turn
wyib	with yarn in back
wyif	with yarn in front
yo	yarn over

Pattern

Note: The two triangles in this pattern are knit identically, making it simple to plan out how you will use your yardage. You will need exactly one half of your yarn for Triangle One and one half of your yarn for Triangle Two.

Triangle One

Using MC, work a Garter Tab cast on as follows.

Garter Tab Cast On: CO 3, knit ten rows, turn work 90 degrees clockwise, then pick up and knit 5 sts along the left edge (one in each garter ridge). Turn work 90 degrees, then pick up 3 sts along the CO edge. [11 sts]

Set-Up Row (WS): Sl1p wyif, k2, pm, k2, pm, p1, pm, k2, pm, k3.

Section 1: Garter

Row 1 (RS): Sl1p wyif, k2, sm, yo, k to m, yo, sm, k1, sm, yo, k to m, yo, sm, k3. [4 sts inc]

Row 2 (WS): Sl1p wyif, k2, sm, k to m, sm, p1, sm, k to m, sm, k3.

Rep Rows 1 and 2 an additional 39 times. End after completing a WS row. [171 sts]

Break MC, leaving a 6-inch (15-cm) tail.

Section 2: Ribbing

Join CC1.

Row 1 (RS): Sl1p wyif, k2, sm, yo, k to m, yo, sm, k1, sm, yo, k to m, yo, sm, k3. [4 sts inc; 175 sts]

Row 2 (WS): Sl1p wyif, k2, sm, k to m, sm, p1, sm, k to m, sm, k3.

Row 3 (RS): Sl1p wyif, k2, sm, (yo, k2tog) rep to m, yo, sm, k1, sm, yo, (ssk, yo) rep to m, sm, k3. [2 sts inc; 177 sts]

Row 4 (WS): Sl1p wyif, k2, sm, k to m, sm, p1, sm, k to m, sm, k3.

Row 5 (RS): Sl1p wyif, k2, sm, yo, p1, (k1, p1) rep to m, yo, sm, k1, sm, yo, p1, (k1, p1) rep to m, yo, sm, k3. [4 sts inc; 181 sts]

Row 6 (WS): Sl1p wyif, k2, sm, p1, (k1, p1) rep to m, sm, p1, sm, p1 (k1, p1) rep to m, sm, k3.

Row 7 (RS): Sl1p wyif, k2, sm, yo, k1, (p1, k1) rep to m, yo, sm, k1, sm, yo, k1, (p1, k1) rep to m, yo, sm, k3. [4 sts inc; 185 sts]

Row 8 (WS): Sl1p wyif, k2, sm, k1, (p1, k1) rep to m, sm, p1, sm, k1 (p1, k1), rep to m, sm, k3.

Rep Rows 5–8 once more. [193 sts]

Row 9 (RS): Sl1p wyif, k2, sm, yo, k to m, yo, sm, k1, sm, yo, k to m, yo, sm, k3. [4 sts inc; 197 sts]

Row 10 (WS): Sl1p wyif, k2, sm, k to m, sm, p1, sm, k to m, sm, k3.

Row 11 (RS): Sl1p wyif, k2, sm, (yo, k2tog) rep to 1 st before m, yo, k1, yo, sm, k1, sm, yo, k1, yo, (ssk, yo) rep to m, sm, k3. [4 sts inc; 201 sts]

In the following row, you will remove both of the outer stitch markers. The two central stitch markers will stay in place.

Row 12 (WS): Sl1p wyif, k2, rm, k to m, sm, p1, sm, k to m, rm, k3.

Break CC1, leaving a 6-inch (15-cm) tail.

Rep Rows 5 and 6 an additional 95 times. You should have 123 sts on your needles [103 ribbing sts and 20 border sts]. You should have 2 ribbing sts remaining before the first central st marker.

You will now begin working a short wedge.

Row 7 (RS): Sl1k wyib, k17, w&t.

Row 8 (WS): P all.

Row 9 (RS): Sl1k wyib, k until 1 st before last wrapped st, w&t.

Row 10 (WS): P all.

Rep Rows 9 and 10 an additional fifteen times, end after completing a WS row. There will be 2 sts between the last wrapped st and the end of the row. You have completed the first short row wedge.

> Note: See page 184 for information on how to work Wrap & Turn Short Rows.

Row 11 (RS): Sl1k wyib, k18 working wraps together with wrapped sts as you come to them, ssk (1 st from the border with 1 st from the ribbing), turn work. [1 st dec; 102 ribbing sts and 20 border sts]

Row 12 (WS): Sl1p wyif, p to end.

In the following row, you will remove the first central st marker before turning your work.

Row 13 (RS): Sl1k wyib, (k2tog, yo) 9 times, ssk (1 st from the border with 1 st from the ribbing), rm, turn work. [1 st dec; 101 ribbing sts and 20 border sts]

Row 14 (WS): Sl1p wyif, p to end.

In the following row, you will remove the second central st marker before turning your work.

Row 15 (RS): Sl1k wyib, k18, ssk (1 st from the border with 1 st from the ribbing section), rm, turn work. [1 st dec; 100 ribbing sts and 20 border sts]

Row 16 (WS): Sl1p wyif, p to end.

Section 3: Attached Rainbow Border

With the RS facing you, join CC2 and, using the Cable cast on method (see page 177), CO 20 sts to your LH needle (in front of the last row of Section 2 sts). You will now have 221 sts on your needles (201 ribbing section sts and 20 new border sts).

Row 1 (RS): Sl1k wyib, k18, ssk (1 st from the border with 1 st from the ribbing section), turn work. [1 st dec; 200 ribbing sts and 20 border sts]

Row 2 (WS): Sl1p wyif, k to end.

Row 3 (RS): Rep Row 1. [1 st dec; 199 ribbing sts and 20 border sts]

Row 4 (WS): Rep Row 2.

Row 5 (RS): Sl1k wyib, k18, ssk (1 st from the border with 1 st from the ribbing), turn work. [1 st dec; 198 ribbing sts and 20 border sts]

Row 6 (WS): Sl1p wyif, p to end.

Row 17 (RS): Sl1k wyib, (ssk, yo) 9 times, ssk (1 st from the border with 1 st from the ribbing), turn work. [1 st dec; 99 ribbing sts and 20 border sts]

Row 18 (WS): Sl1p wyif, p to end.

You will now begin working the second short wedge.

Row 19 (RS): Sl1k wyib, k1, w&t.

Row 20 (WS): P all.

Row 21 (RS): Sl1k wyib, k to wrapped st, pick up and k wrapped st, w&t.

Row 22 (WS): P all.

Rep Rows 21 and 22 an additional fifteen times. End after completing a WS row. There will be 18 sts between the last wrapped st and the end of the row. You have completed the second short row wedge.

Row 23 (RS): Sl1k wyib, k18 working the wrap together with the wrapped st as you come to it, ssk (1 st from the border with 1 st from the ribbing), turn work. [1 st dec; 98 ribbing sts and 20 border sts]

Row 24 (WS): Sl1p wyif, p to end.

Row 25 (RS): Sl1k wyib, k18, ssk (1 st from the border with 1 st from the ribbing), turn work. [1 st dec; 97 ribbing sts and 20 border sts]

Row 26 (WS): Sl1p wyif, p to end.

Rep Rows 25 and 26 until you have a total of 23 sts on your needles. [3 ribbing sts and 20 border sts]

Work Row 25 once more. [1 st dec; 2 ribbing sts and 20 border sts]

Next Row (WS): Sl1p wyif, k to end.

Next Row (RS): Sl1k wyib, k18, ssk (1 st from the border with 1 st from the ribbing), turn work. [1 st dec; 1 ribbing st and 20 border sts]

Next Row (WS): Sl1p wyif, k to end.

Next Row (RS): Sl1k wyib, k18, ssk (1 st from the border with 1 st from the ribbing), turn work. [1 st dec; 20 border sts]

Next Row (WS): BO all sts knitwise. Break CC2, leaving a 6-inch (15-cm) tail.

Section 4: Ribbing

With the RS facing you, using CC1, pick up and knit 235 sts along the slipped st edge of the attached border. You will be picking up one st for each slipped st along the Attached Rainbow Border.

Next Row (WS): Sl1p wyif, k2, pm, k114, pm, p1, pm, k114, pm, k3.

Row 1 (RS): Sl1p wyif, k2, sm, (yo, k2tog) rep to m, yo, sm, k1, sm, yo, (ssk, yo) rep to m, sm, k3. [2 sts inc; 237 sts]

Row 2 (WS): Sl1p wyif, k2, sm, k to m, sm, p1, sm, k to m, sm, k3.

Row 3 (RS): Sl1p wyif, k2, sm, yo, (p1, k1) rep to 1 st before m, p1, yo, sm, k1, sm, yo, p1, (k1, p1) rep to m, yo, sm, k3. [4 sts inc; 241 sts]

Row 4 (WS): Sl1p wyif, k2, sm, (p1, k1) rep to 1 st before m, p1, sm, p1, sm, p1, (k1, p1) rep to m, sm, k3.

Row 5 (RS): Sl1p wyif, k2, sm, yo, (k1, p1) rep to 1 st before m, k1, yo, sm, k1, sm, yo, k1, (p1, k1) rep to m, yo, sm, k3. [4 sts inc; 245 sts]

Row 6 (WS): Sl1p wyif, k2, sm, (k1, p1) rep to 1 st before m, k1, sm, p1, sm, k1, (p1, k1) rep to m, sm, k3.

Rep Rows 3–6 once more. [253 sts]

Row 7 (RS): Sl1p wyif, k2, sm, yo, k to m, yo, sm, k1, sm, yo, k to m, yo, sm, k3. [4 sts inc; 257 sts]

Row 8 (WS): Sl1p wyif, k2, sm, k to m, sm, p1, sm, k to m, sm, k3.

Row 9 (RS): Sl1p wyif, k2, sm, (yo, k2tog) rep to 1 st before m, yo, k1, yo, sm, k1, sm, yo, k1, yo, (ssk, yo) rep to m, sm, k3. [4 sts inc; 261 sts]

Row 10 (WS): Sl1p wyif, k2, sm, k to m, sm, p1, sm, k to m, sm, k3.

Break CC1, leaving a 6-inch (15-cm) tail.

Section 5: Garter

Join MC.

Row 1 (RS): Sl1p wyif, k2, sm, yo, k to m, yo, sm, k1, sm, yo, k to m, yo, sm, k3. [4 sts inc; 265 sts]

Row 2 (WS): Sl1p wyif, k2, sm, k to m, sm, p1, sm, k to m, sm, k3.

Rep Rows 1 and 2 an additional eighteen times. End after completing a WS row. [337 sts]

Note: If you would like to adjust the final stitch count to better suit your yardage, please see the "Adjusting Your Final Stitch Count" section on page 121.

Section 6: Bind Off

BO 169 sts using the following Stretchy Bind Off, or a stretchy bind off of your choice. Break MC, leaving a 6-inch (15-cm) tail. Place the remaining 168 sts on a piece of scrap yarn or leave them on a spare set of needles and set aside. Remove stitch markers as you come to them.

Stretchy Bind Off: K1, (k1, slip 2 st just worked to left needle, k2tog through the back loop) rep to end.

Note: If you are knitting a one-triangle shawl, BO all sts using the Stretchy Bind Off and proceed to the Finishing section.

Triangle Two

Rep Triangle One. Triangle Two will be worked identically to Triangle One. Once you have worked the Stretchy Bind Off, do not place your remaining sts on hold and do not break your yarn. Instead, leave them on your needles for the following section.

Joining the Triangles

Place the held sts from Triangle One onto a second set of knitting needles. Place both triangles on the floor so that the live sts meet. You will use the live yarn from Triangle Two to join the two triangles together. With the WS of both triangles facing each other and the RS facing out, use a three-needle bind off to BO all sts (see page 180). This will create a garter ridge on the RS of the shawl. I recommend working this BO loosely. Break MC, leaving a 6-inch (15-cm) tail.

Note: You can use the construction image on page 116 as a reference.

Finishing

Weave in all ends. For the best results, be sure to wet block your finished shawl. Soak the shawl in cold water, squeezing to remove air bubbles. Squeeze out the water, but do not wring. Roll the shawl in a dry towel, burrito-style, and press on it to remove excess water. Lay the shawl flat to dry, using a measuring tape to be sure it is laid out with the correct dimensions.

Adjusting Your Final Stitch Count

You can easily adjust the number of garter rows worked in Section 5 to maximize your yardage. You will need one half of your MC yardage for Triangle One and the other half for Triangle Two. To maximize your MC yardage, rep Garter Rows 1 and 2 until you are ready to BO. End after completing a WS row.

Note: If you are trying to use every last bit of your yarn, plan to use approximately 1 inch (2.5 cm) of yarn for each stitch you BO.

Step 1: Count how many sts you have on your needles. It should be an odd number of sts.

Step 2: Subtract 1 from your total.

For example, if you have 357 sts on your needles, you would subtract 1 from 357. This would be 356.

Step 3: Divide this number in half.

In this example, half of 356 is 178.

Step 4: Add 1 to this number and BO this number of sts.

For this example, 178 + 1 = 179. Therefore, you would BO 179 sts.

Step 5: Place the remaining sts on hold.

The remaining 178 sts would be placed on a piece of scrap yarn or a spare set of needles.

Step 6: Make a note of these numbers so you can work Triangle Two identically to Triangle One.

Flipped Shawlette

Skill Level: Adventurous Beginner

The Flipped Shawlette is half the fuss of a full shawl and double the fun. This little knit gives you the chance to play with not one but two self-striping colorways. The pattern is a simple pattern flipped in two directions. While this shawlette has the appearance of intarsia, there is no intarsia involved at all. No more tangled yarn cakes! Using a simple combination of picking up stitches and decreases, this shawlette knits up quickly and has a dramatic impact.

Construction

The Flipped Shawlette is knit flat from end to end. The first section is knit in your main color. Then the second section is picked up along the length of the main color section and knit flat in a mirror image of the first section.

Maximum Stitches Used for a Self-Striping Row: 27

Sizes

One Size

See the Finished Measurements.

Yarn

- Fingering weight yarn, Canon Hand Dyes Charles Merino
- (80% superwash merino and 20% nylon, 400 yards / 3.5 ounces [365 m / 100 g])
- Sample shown in "Raven Claw Polar Opposites" (MC, gray with blue stripes and CC, blue with gray stripes)
- 1 50-g skein of MC and 1 50-g skein of CC
- **Main Color:** 200 yards (183 m)
- **Contrasting Color:** 200 yards (183 m)

Yarn Notes

This pattern was knit using a special kind of self-striping yarn called "Polar Opposites." This self-striping is dyed in two 50-g mini skeins with a matching but opposite stripe sequence.

Needles

US 7 (4.5 mm) 36-inch (80-cm) circular needles, or as required to meet gauge

Gauge

20 stitches and 24 rows = 4 inches (10 cm) in stockinette stitch after blocking

Notions

- Scissors
- Tapestry needle
- Blocking wires or pins
- Tape measure

Finished Measurements

A. **Length:** 48 inches (122 cm)

B. **Width:** 12 inches (30.5 cm)

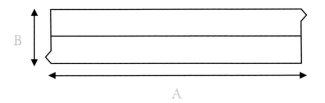

Abbreviations

BO	bind off
CC	contrasting color
cdd	central double decrease
CO	cast on
dec	decrease
k	knit
k2tog	knit two together
MC	main color
p	purl
pm	place marker
rep	repeat
RS	right side
sl1p	slip one purlwise
st(s)	stitch(es)
WS	wrong side
wyib	with yarn in back
wyif	with yarn in front
yo	yarn over

Pattern

Section 1

Using MC, CO 27 sts.

Row 1 (RS): Sl1p wyif, k26.

Row 2 (WS): Sl1p wyif, k26.

Rep Rows 1 and 2 once more.

Row 3 (RS): Sl1p wyib, k1, yo, k5, cdd, k5, yo, k5, yo, k3, k2tog, k2.

Row 4 (WS): Sl1p wyif, p26.

Rep Rows 3 and 4 until Section 1 measures 47.5 inches (120.5 cm) or 0.5 inches (1.25 cm) less than your target length. End after completing a WS row. You will need approximately 5 yards (4.5 m) of yarn to complete the remainder of Section 1.

Row 5 (RS): Sl1p wyif, k26.

Row 6 (WS): Sl1p wyif, k26.

Rep Rows 5 and 6 once more. Rep Row 5 once more. BO all sts knitwise on a WS row. Break MC, leaving a 6-inch (15-cm) tail.

Connection Stitches

In this section, you will be picking up sts along the edge of Section 1. The stitches that you pick up in this section will allow you to invisibly connect Section 1 and Section 2 without using intarsia.

Lay Section 1 flat in front of you with the RS facing up. The side edge should be facing away from you. The CO edge will be at the left end, and the BO edge will be at the right end. Using CC, pick up and knit 1 st for every row along the upper edge of Section 1 (Fig. 1 below).

Pick up sts along the upper edge

Cast On Edge — Bind Off Edge

1

Note: You will be picking up sts along the edge where you worked the "k2tog," not the edge where you worked the "yo."

Pick up and knit approximately 175 sts along the upper edge.

Section 2

Using the Cable cast on method (see page 177), CO an additional 26 sts. You should now have 201 sts on your needles (175 connection sts and 26 CO sts). These 26 sts are your Section 2 sts.

Set-Up Row (WS): Sl1p wyif, k24, p2tog (1 connection st with 1 st from Section 2). [1 st dec]

Row 1 (RS): Sl1p wyib, k25.

Row 2 (WS): Sl1p wyif, k24, p2tog (1 connection st with 1 st from section two). [1 st dec]

Rep Rows 1 and 2 once more. [1 st dec]

Row 3 (RS): Sl1p wyib, k2tog, k3, yo, k5, yo, k5, cdd, k5, yo, k2.

Row 4 (WS): Sl1p wyif, p24, p2tog (1 connection st with 1 st from Section 2). [1 st dec]

Rep Rows 3 and 4 until you have 29 sts on your needles. End after completing a WS row. Work Row 3 once more.

Next Row (WS): Sl1p wyif, k24, p2tog. [1 st dec]

Row 5 (RS): Sl1p wyib, k25.

Row 6 (WS): Sl1p wyif, k24, p2tog. [1 st dec]

Rep Rows 5 and 6 once more [1 st dec; 26 sts remaining]. BO all sts purlwise on a RS row. Break MC, leaving a 6-inch (15-cm) tail.

Finishing

Weave in all ends. For the best results, be sure to wet block your finished shawlette. Soak the shawlette in cold water, squeezing to remove air bubbles. Squeeze out the water, but do not wring. Roll the shawlette in a dry towel, burrito-style, and press on it to remove excess water. Lay the shawlette flat to dry, using a measuring tape to be sure it is laid out with the correct dimensions. Use blocking pins or wires to open up the simple lace in this shawlette.

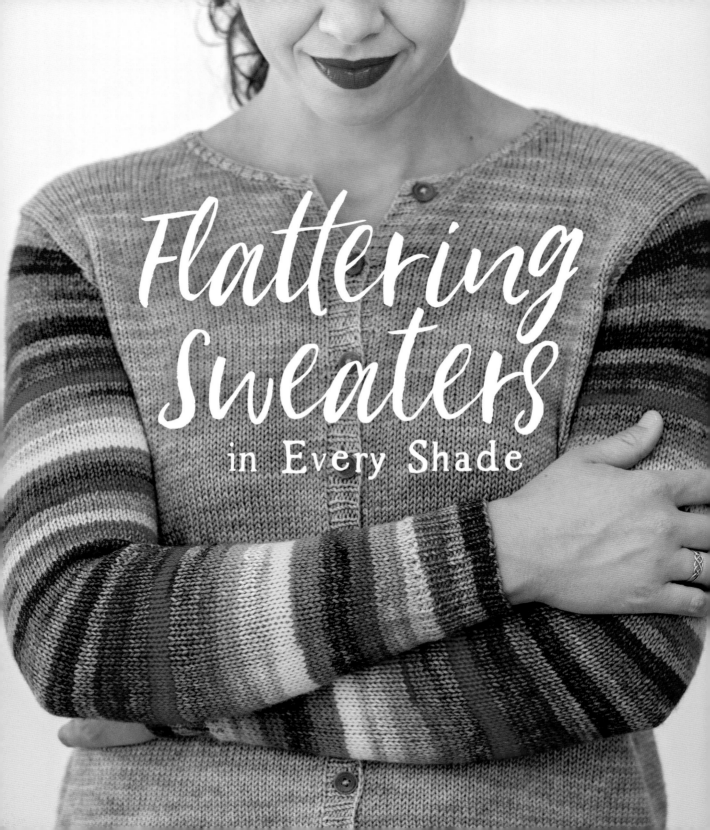

When I was a kid, I was never satisfied with my crayon box. The 8-count, 12-count and even 24-count boxes of waxy crayons always left me wanting more, and so, for my eighth birthday, I asked for a big box of 120 crayons (the one with the crayon sharpener in the back). I still remember using the cornflower blue and thinking, "This is the blue I've been missing my whole life." The sweaters on the following pages are the yarn equivalent of that big box of colors. With long stretches of uninterrupted knitting, these cardigans and pullovers will give you the chance to show off every color in the box—or skein, that is.

Kiddo-me knew that the path to happiness is full of options, and I still believe this today. In these pages, you will find tips and guided examples that will help you modify your sweater so that you can make choices that flatter your body. Look for advice on when and how to eliminate waist shaping in the Sock Arms Cardigan (page 129). Use the step-by-step instructions for changing the circumference of your sleeves in the Drop a Rainbow Pullover (page 161). Having these choices—and lots of others—throughout this chapter will ensure that you don't spend hours knitting a sweater that looks glorious on the blocking mats but doesn't feel great on your body.

Once you find the right fit for you, all of the designs in this chapter give you the opportunity to enjoy long stretches of your favorite self-striping yarn. In these pages, you will use attached edging, short rows and relaxing stockinette to create sweaters that use your best self-striping yarns thoughtfully. Don't settle for a ho-hum sweater with a humdrum fit. Dig into your stash and find that incredible skein of self-striping you have been hiding away for something special, because, whether you are 8, 38 or 68 years old, everyone deserves to use the big box of crayons.

Sock Arms Cardigan
Skill Level: Intermediate

Have you ever heard of second sock syndrome? If you aren't a sock knitter, maybe you haven't. Second sock syndrome hits when you have just finished knitting your first beautiful sock. You stop, you admire your handiwork, you think about the hours of work you poured into that lovely sock. Then you realize that you have to do it all over again. The second sock is just harder to knit. Well, if you are a sweater knitter, you know that it is so much worse with sleeves. Second sleeve syndrome is REAL. After knitting a fun, engaging sweater body, most sleeves are boring tubes of solid-colored dullness. Well, not these sleeves! The Sock Arms Cardigan was designed to use your favorite self-striping yarn where you need it the most—on the sleeves. In this sweater, you will race through the body so you can knit rainbow sleeves. Finally . . . FUN SLEEVES!

Construction

This cardigan is knit seamlessly from the top down. The yoke and body are worked first. After completing the body of the sweater, the sleeves are picked up and worked in the round from underarm to wrist, beginning with a sleeve cap shaped using the German Short Rows method (see page 184). The collar is picked up and worked flat. Lastly, the button bands are picked up and worked flat.

Maximum Stitches Used for a Self-Striping Round: 60 (68, 80, 90, **98, 108, 114,** 116, 118, 120)

Sizes

Adult XS (S, M, L, **XL, 2XL, 3XL,** 4XL, 5XL, 6XL)

See the Finished Measurements on page 130 to choose your size.

NOTE: Throughout this pattern you will find that **sizes XL, 2XL and 3XL** appear in bold type. Use this indicator to help you easily find your size as you navigate the pattern. Want to make sure you get the right fit? Check out the "Tips on Modifying Your Sweater" section on page 137 to get the most out of your Sock Arms Cardigan.

Yarn

- Sport weight yarn, Must Stash Sport Sock

- (80% superwash merino and 20% nylon, 328 yards / 3.5 ounces [300 m / 100 g])

- Samples shown in "Reflection" (MC, gray), "Mordor Fun Run" (CC, self-striping), "Moroccan" (MC, brown) and "Bohemian Rainbow" (CC, self-striping)

- 2 (2, 2, 2, **2, 3, 3,** 3, 3, 3) skeins of MC and 1 (1, 2, 2, **2, 2, 2,** 2, 3, 3) skeins of CC

- **Main Color:** 650 (695, 750, 800, **895, 1010, 1120,** 1220, 1380, 1560) yards / [595 (636, 686, 732, **818, 924, 1024,** 1116, 1262, 1426) m]

- **Contrasting Color:** 330 (355, 425, 475, **525, 574, 615,** 625, 675, 715) yards / [302 (325, 389, 434, **480, 525, 562,** 572, 617, 654) m]

Yarn Notes

This pattern was knit using a three-ply sport weight yarn to create a dense, warm fabric. Using sport weight yarn at this gauge will give you a snuggly, warm cardigan that you can layer over your favorite outfit in any weather. If you prefer a lighter fabric, consider using a fingering weight yarn at the same gauge.

Needles

US 4 (3.5 mm) 32-inch (80-cm) circular needles (length as appropriate for your size), or as required to meet gauge

US 3 (3.25 mm) 32-inch (80-cm) circular needles (length as appropriate for your size)

DPNs or needles for small circumference in the smaller size needles

Gauge

24 stitches and 32 rounds = 4 inches (10 cm) in stockinette stitch on LARGER needles after blocking

Notions

- 10 (10, 10, 11, **11, 11, 11,** 11, 11, 11) [½-inch (1.25-cm)] buttons
- 2 stitch markers
- Scissors
- Tapestry needle
- Scrap yarn
- Tape measure

Finished Measurements

Samples shown in size M with 2 inches (7.5 cm) of positive ease at the bust, and size 2XL with 4 inches (10 cm) of positive ease at the bust. I recommend 2 to 4 inches (5 to 10 cm) of ease at the bust for this cardigan.

A. **Bust:** 30 (34, 38, 42, **46, 50, 54,** 58, 62, 66) inches / [75 (85, 95, 105, **115, 125, 135,** 145, 155, 165) cm]

B. **Hips:** 32.75 (36.75, 40.75, 44.75, **48.75, 52.75, 56.75,** 60.75, 64.75, 68.75) inches / [82 (92, 102, 112, **122, 132, 142,** 152, 162, 172) cm]

C. **Length of Body (Hem to Underarm):** 16.5 (16.5, 16.5, 17, **17, 17.5, 18,** 18, 18, 18) inches / [41.5 (41.5, 41.5, 42.5, **42.5, 44, 45,** 45, 45, 45) cm]

D. **Sleeve Circumference:** 10 (11.5, 13.5, 15, **16.5, 18, 19,** 19.5, 19.75, 20) inches / [25 (28.5, 33.5, 37.5, **41, 45, 47.5,** 48.5, 49, 50) cm]

E. **Wrist Circumference:** 6.75 (7, 7.5, 7.75, **8, 8.5, 9,** 9.5, 9.5, 9.5) inches / [17 (17.5, 19, 19.5, **20, 21.5, 22.5,** 24, 24, 24) cm]

F. **Sleeve Length:** 17 (17.25, 17.5, 17.5, **17.75, 17.75, 18,** 18, 18, 18) inches / [42.5 (43, 44, 44, **44.5, 44.5, 45,** 45, 45, 45) cm]

G. **Yoke Depth:** 6.25 (6.75, 7.5, 8, **8.5, 9, 9.5,** 9.75, 10, 10.25) inches / [16 (17, 19, 20, **21.5, 22.5, 24,** 24.5, 25, 25.5) cm]

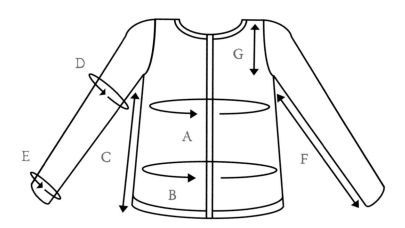

Abbreviations	
BO	bind off
BOR	beginning of round
CC	contrasting color
CO	cast on
dec	decrease
DPNs	double pointed needles
DS	double stitch
inc	increase
k	knit
k2tog	knit two together
m	marker
MC	main color
m1L	make one left
m1R	make one right
p	purl
pm	place marker
rep	repeat
RH	right-hand
RS	right side
sl	slip
sl1k	slip one knitwise
sl1p	slip one purlwise
sm	slip marker
ssk	slip, slip, knit
st(s)	stitch(es)
WS	wrong side
wyib	with yarn in back
wyif	with yarn in front

Pattern

Back Right Shoulder

Using LARGER needles and MC, CO 18 (20, 21, 22, **22, 25, 28,** 30, 32, 35) sts.

Row 1 (RS): K all.

Row 2 (WS): P all.

In this section, you will be casting on sts for the back of the neck. Use the Cable cast on for these CO sts. For a tutorial on the Cable cast on, see page 177.

Row 3 (RS): CO 3, k to end. [3 sts inc]

Row 4 (WS): P all.

Rep Rows 3 and 4 until you have 27 (29, 33, 34, **34, 40, 43,** 45, 47, 50) sts on your needles. End after completing a WS row. Break yarn, leaving a 6-inch (15-cm) tail. Place sts on hold.

Back Left Shoulder

Using LARGER needles and MC, CO 18 (20, 21, 22, **22, 25, 28,** 30, 32, 35) sts.

Row 1 (RS): K all.

Row 2 (WS): P all.

Row 3 (RS): K all.

Row 4 (WS): CO 3, p to end. [3 sts inc]

Row 5 (RS): K all.

Rep Rows 4 and 5 until you have 27 (29, 33, 34, **34, 40, 43,** 45, 47, 50) sts on your needles. End after completing a WS row. Do not break yarn.

Back of the Neck Join & Back Yoke

Joining Row (RS): K to end, CO 12 (18, 18, 26, **34, 32, 34,** 40, 46, 52) sts. Place the Back Right Shoulder on your needle with the RS facing you. K to end. [12 (18, 18, 26, **34, 32, 34,** 40, 46, 52) sts inc; 66 (76, 84, 94, **102, 112, 120,** 130, 140, 152) sts total]

Work in stockinette stitch (k the RS rows, p the WS rows) until your Back Yoke measures approximately 3.5 (3.5, 4, 4, **4.25, 4.5, 4.5,** 4.5, 4.75, 5) inches [9 (9, 10, 10, **11, 11.5, 11.5,** 11.5, 12, 12.5) cm] from the top of the shoulder CO. End after completing a WS row. You will now begin increasing along the underarms.

Row 1 (RS): K1, m1R, k to last st, m1L, k1. [2 sts inc]

Row 2 (WS): P all.

Row 3 (RS): K all.

Row 4 (WS): P all.

Rep Rows 1–4 until you have 72 (84, 92, 104, **112, 122, 132,** 142, 152, 164) sts. End after completing Row 4.

Row 5 (RS): K1, m1R, k to last st, m1L, k1. [2 sts inc]

Row 6 (WS): P all.

Rep Rows 5 and 6 until you have 82 (94, 104, 116, **126, 138, 148,** 160, 170, 182) sts. End after completing a WS row. Break yarn, leaving a 6-inch (15-cm) tail.

Place your Back Yoke sts on a piece of scrap yarn.

Front Right Yoke

Start at the shoulder edge. With the RS facing you and using LARGER needles and MC, pick up and knit 18 (20, 21, 22, **22, 25, 28,** 30, 32, 35) sts along the Back Right Shoulder CO edge.

Note: When picking up sts along the CO edge, pick up the Front Shoulder sts directly into the Back Shoulder CO sts, not in between.

Work five rows in stockinette stitch (k the RS rows, p the WS rows). End after completing a WS row. You will now begin increasing along the neckline.

Row 1 (RS): K to last st, m1R, k1. [1 st inc]

Row 2 (WS): P all.

Rep Rows 1 and 2 until you have 20 (23, 25, 27, **31, 34, 36,** 39, 41, 44) sts on your needles. End after completing a WS row.

Row 3 (RS): K to last st, m1R, k1. [1 st inc]

Row 4 (WS): P1, m1R purlwise, p to end. [1 st inc]

Rep Rows 3 and 4 until you have 24 (29, 33, 37, **41, 46, 48,** 53, 55, 60) sts. End after completing a WS row.

Front of the Neck CO Row (RS): K to end, CO 6 (6, 6, 7, **7, 7, 9,** 9, 12, 13) sts. [6 (6, 6, 7, **7, 7, 9,** 9, 12, 13) sts inc; 30 (35, 39, 44, **48, 53, 57,** 62, 67, 73) sts total]

Work in stockinette stitch (k the RS rows, p the WS rows) until the Front Right Yoke measures 3.5 (3.5, 4, 4, **4.25, 4.5, 4.5,** 4.5, 4.75, 5) inches [9 (9, 10, 10, **11, 11.5, 11.5,** 11.5, 12, 12.5) cm] from the top of the shoulder. End after completing a WS row. You will now begin increasing along the underarm.

Row 5 (RS): K1, m1R, k to end. [1 st inc]

Row 6 (WS): P all.

Row 7 (RS): K all.

Row 8 (WS): P all.

Work Rows 5–8 until you have 33 (39, 43, 49, **53, 58, 63,** 68, 73, 79) sts. End after completing Row 8.

Row 9 (RS): K1, m1R, k to end. [1 st inc]

Row 10 (WS): P all.

Rep Rows 9 and 10 until you have 38 (44, 49, 55, **60, 66, 71,** 77, 82, 88) sts. End after completing a WS Row. Break yarn, leaving a 6-inch (15-cm) tail.

Place your Front Right Yoke sts on a piece of scrap yarn.

Front Left Yoke

Start at the neckline edge. With the RS facing you and using LARGER needles and MC, pick up and knit 18 (20, 21, 22, **22, 25, 28,** 30, 32, 35) sts along the Back Left Shoulder CO edge.

Work five rows in stockinette stitch (k the RS rows, p the WS rows). End after completing a WS row. You will now begin increasing along the neckline.

Row 1 (RS): K1, m1L, k to end. [1 st inc]

Row 2 (WS): P all.

Rep Rows 1 and 2 until you have 20 (23, 25, 27, **31, 34, 36,** 39, 41, 44) sts on your needles. End after completing a RS row.

Next Row (WS): P to last st, m1L purlwise, p1. [1 st inc]

Row 3 (RS): K1, m1L, k to end. [1 st inc]

Row 4 (WS): P to last st, m1L purlwise, p1. [1 st inc]

Rep Rows 3 and 4 until you have 24 (29, 33, 37, **41, 46, 48,** 53, 55, 60) sts. End after completing a RS row.

Front of the Neck CO Row (WS): P to end, CO 6 (6, 6, 7, **7, 7, 9,** 9, 12, 13) sts. [6 (6, 6, 7, **7, 7, 9,** 9, 12, 13) sts inc; 30 (35, 39, 44, **48, 53, 57,** 62, 67, 73) sts total]

Work in stockinette stitch (k the RS rows, p the WS rows) until the Front Left Yoke measures 3.5 (3.5, 4, 4, **4.25, 4.5, 4.5,** 4.5, 4.75, 5) inches [9 (9, 10, 10, **11, 11.5, 11.5,** 11.5, 12, 12.5) cm] from the top of the shoulder. End after completing a WS row. You will now begin increasing along the underarm.

Row 5 (RS): K to last st, m1L, k1. [1 st inc]

Row 6 (WS): P all.

Row 7 (RS): K all.

Row 8 (WS): P all.

Work Rows 5–8 until you have 33 (39, 43, 49, **53, 58, 63,** 68, 73, 79) sts.

Row 9 (RS): K to last st, m1L, k1. [1 st inc]

Row 10 (WS): P all.

Rep Rows 9 and 10 until you have 38 (44, 49, 55, **60, 66, 71,** 77, 82, 88) sts. End after completing a WS Row.

Joining the Front & Back Yokes

Joining Row (RS): K across 38 (44, 49, 55, **60, 66, 71,** 77, 82, 88) Front Left Yoke sts, CO 4 (4, 5, 5, **6, 6, 7,** 7, 8, 8) underarm sts, pm, CO 4 (4, 5, 5, **6, 6, 7,** 7, 8, 8) additional underarm sts, k across 82 (94, 104, 116, **126, 138, 148,** 160, 170, 182) Back Yoke sts, CO 4 (4, 5, 5, **6, 6, 7,** 7, 8, 8) underarm sts, pm, CO 4 (4, 5, 5, **6, 6, 7,** 7, 8, 8) additional underarm sts, k across 38 (44, 49, 55, **60, 66, 71,** 77, 82, 88) Front Right Yoke sts.

You should now have 174 (198, 222, 246, **270, 294, 318,** 342, 366, 390) sts on your needles.

Body

Work in stockinette stitch (k the RS rows, p the WS rows) until the Body measures 2 inches (5 cm) from the CO underarm sts.

Body Increase Row (RS): (K to 1 st before m, m1R, k1, sm, k1, m1L) 2 times, k to end. [4 sts inc]

Work in stockinette stitch for nine rows. End after completing a WS row.

Work the previous ten rows until you have 190 (214, 238, 262, **286, 310, 334,** 358, 382, 406) sts.

Work in stockinette stitch until your work measures approximately 15.25 (15.25, 15.25, 15.75, **15.75, 16.25, 16.75,** 16.75, 16.75, 16.75) inches [38.5 (38.5, 38.5, 39.5, **39.5, 41, 42,** 42, 42, 42) cm] from the underarm CO or 1.25 inches (3 cm) less than your desired length. End after completing a WS row. If you would like to add length to your sweater, do so here.

> Note: Changes to the length of your sweater will result in changes to your final yardage.

Change to SMALLER needles.

Work 1x1 ribbing (k1, p1) until the Body measures approximately 16.5 (16.5, 16.5, 17, **17, 17.5, 18,** 18, 18, 18) inches [41.5 (41.5, 41.5, 42.5, **42.5, 42.5, 44,** 45, 45, 45) cm] from the underarm CO or desired length. End after completing a WS row. BO all sts in pattern. Break yarn, leaving a 6-inch (15-cm) tail.

Sleeves (both worked identically)

> Note: Seamless set-in sleeves are new to many knitters. When working a set-in sleeve, you may notice that the Anchor Round looks loose after completing the sleeve cap. This is not an error in knitting or in the pattern. This round tends to loosen naturally as you work the short rows for the sleeve cap. To get a clean sleeve cap, see the "Perfecting the Set-In Sleeve" section on page 136 after you complete your sleeves.

Using MC and LARGER needles for small circumference knitting, pick up 60 (68, 80, 90, **98, 108, 114,** 116, 118, 120) sts around the armhole, as follows:

Anchor Round: Pick up and knit 30 (34, 40, 45, **49, 54, 57,** 58, 59, 60) sts evenly between the middle of the underarm and the shoulder seam. Pick up and knit 30 (34, 40, 45, **49, 54, 57,** 58, 59, 60) sts evenly between the shoulder seam and the middle of the underarm. Place a BOR marker. Break MC, leaving a 6-inch (15-cm) tail. Place a removable marker after st 10 (12, 14, 15, **17, 18, 19,** 20, 21, 22). Place another removable marker after st 50 (56, 66, 75, **81, 90, 95,** 96, 97, 98). You should have 40 (44, 52, 60, **64, 72, 76,** 76, 76, 76) sts between the 2 removable markers.

You will now begin short row shaping the sleeve cap.

Row 1 (RS): Sl20 (23, 27, 30, **33, 36, 38,** 39, 39, 40) purlwise, join CC, k21 (23, 27, 31, **33, 37, 39,** 39, 41, 41), turn work.

Row 2 (WS): DS, p21 (23, 27, 31, **33, 37, 39,** 39, 41, 41), turn work.

Row 3 (RS): DS, k to last DS, resolve DS, k1, turn work.

Row 4 (WS): DS, p to last DS, resolve DS, p1, turn work.

Work Rows 3 and 4 until the last st next to the second removable marker has been worked as a DS. In the following row, you will work a DS on the last st next to the first removable marker.

Next Row (RS): DS, knit to the beginning of the row, resolving all DS sts as you come to them. There will be one remaining DS to resolve on the next round. Remove the removable markers ONLY. Leave the BOR marker in place.

You will now begin working in the round. Knit six rounds.

Sleeve Decrease Round: K1, k2tog, k to last 3 sts, ssk, k1. [2 sts dec]

Knit 10 (7, 5, 4, **3, 3, 3,** 3, 3, 3) rounds.

Rep the previous 11 (8, 6, 5, **4, 4, 4,** 4, 4, 4) rounds until you have 40 (42, 44, 46, **48, 50, 54,** 56, 56, 56) sts.

Work in stockinette stitch (k every round) until the sleeve measures 15 (15.25, 15.5, 15.5, **15.75, 15.75, 16,** 16, 16, 16) inches [37.5 (38, 39, 39, **39.5 39.5, 40.5,** 40.5, 40.5, 40.5) cm] from the underarm or 2 inches (5 cm) less than your desired length.

> **Note:** When using a self-striping yarn, on the first round of each new color, knit all the purl sts in that round. Substituting a knit st for a purl st in the color change rounds will give you a clean color transition. When you have completed the first round of the new color, continue to work the purl sts according to the pattern.

> **Note:** If your self-striping yardage is limited, consider shortening the sleeves or using the MC for your sleeve cuffs.

Change to SMALLER needles. Work 1x1 ribbing (k1, p1) until ribbing measures 2 inches (5 cm), or desired length.

BO all sts in pattern and break yarn, leaving a 6-inch (15-cm) tail.

Collar

Begin with the RS facing you. With SMALLER needles and MC, pick up and knit 6 (6, 6, 7, **7, 7, 9,** 9, 12, 13) sts along the front right CO edge of the neckline, 3 of 4 sts along the slope of the neck, all sts across the back of the neck, 3 of 4 sts along the slope of the neck and 6 (6, 6, 7, **7, 7, 9,** 9, 12, 13) sts along the front left CO edge of the neckline. You will need an odd number of sts on your needles.

Ribbing Row (WS): (P1, k1) rep to last st, p1.

Ribbing Row (RS): (K1, p1) rep to last st, k1.

Work 1x1 ribbing for three rows. End after completing a WS row. BO all sts in pattern. Break yarn, leaving a 6-inch (15-cm) tail.

Right Front Edge Button Band (Buttonhole Side)

Begin at the hem with the RS facing you. With SMALLER needles and MC, pick up and knit 127 (127, 127, 133, **133, 133, 141,** 141, 141, 141) sts.

Ribbing Row (WS): Sl1p wyif, (k1, p1) rep to end.

Ribbing Row (RS): Sl1k wyib, (p1, k1) rep to end.

Work 1x1 ribbing for three rows. End after completing a WS row.

In the following two rows, you will work in pattern (knitting the knit sts and purling the purl sts). You will be binding off sts to create a buttonhole. Binding off sts will leave a st on your RH needle. Leave this st on your RH needle, then continue to work in pattern.

Buttonhole Row (RS): Work 4 (4, 4, 5, **5, 5, 4,** 4, 4, 4) sts in pattern, [BO 2, work 10 (10, 10, 9, **9, 9, 10,** 10, 10, 10) sts in pattern] 9 (9, 9, 10, **10, 10, 10,** 10, 10, 10) times, BO 2, work 4 (4, 4, 6, **6, 6, 5,** 5, 5, 5) sts in pattern.

Buttonhole Row (WS): Work 4 (4, 4, 6, **6, 6, 5,** 5, 5, 5) sts in pattern, [CO 2 at the buttonhole gap, work 11 (11, 11, 10, **10, 10, 11,** 11, 11, 11) sts in pattern] rep 9 (9, 9, 10, **10, 10, 10,** 10, 10, 10) times, CO 2 at the buttonhole gap, work in pattern to end.

Work 1x1 ribbing for two rows. End after completing a WS row. BO all sts in pattern. Break yarn, leaving a 6-inch (15-cm) tail.

Left Front Edge Button Band (Button Side)

Begin at the neckline with the RS facing you. With SMALLER needles and MC, pick up and knit 127 (127, 127, 133, **133, 133, 141,** 141, 141, 141) sts.

Ribbing Row (WS): Sl1p wyif, (k1, p1) rep to end.

Ribbing Row (RS): Sl1k wyib, (p1, k1) rep to end.

Work 1x1 ribbing for a total of seven rows. End on a WS row. BO all sts in pattern. Break yarn, leaving a 6-inch (15-cm) tail.

Finishing

Attach 10 (10, 10, 11, **11, 11, 11,** 11, 11, 11) [½-inch (1.25-cm)] buttons in alignment with the buttonholes. Weave in all ends. For the best results, be sure to wet block your finished sweater. Soak the sweater in cold water, squeezing to remove air bubbles. Squeeze out the water, but do not wring. Roll the sweater in a dry towel, burrito-style, and press on it to remove excess water. Lay the sweater flat to dry, using a measuring tape to be sure it is laid out with the correct dimensions.

Perfecting the Set-In Sleeve

AFTER knitting your sweater and BEFORE weaving in ends, locate the Anchor Round of your sleeve. This round will be knit in the MC and should be easy to spot. If the sts in the Anchor Round look loose, tighten them. You will tighten one half of the sts first and then the other half. Do this by starting at the shoulder seam and working your way down toward the underarm. See the photos on page 146. First, locate the Anchor Round (see Photo 1). Using a tapestry needle, locate the left and right leg of each loose st (see Photo 2). Carefully, pull the right leg of the st to tighten the left side of the st. This will create a long, loose loop (see Photo 3). Pull the left leg of the next st (one st closer to the underarm) to tighten this loop. Then pull the right leg to tighten the left leg.

Continue to work in this manner until you reach the center of the underarm. Turn your pullover inside out and pull the tail of the Anchor Round to tighten the final loose loop. Repeat this process for the second half of the Anchor Round.

Tips on Modifying Your Sweater

Note: Any modifications to the pattern will result in changes to your final yardage.

If you do not want waist shaping:

If you tend to wear your cardigan open rather than keeping it buttoned, you may find the waist shaping unnecessary. Waist shaping will add additional fabric that is wonderful for hugging your curves when the sweater is buttoned. However, this extra fabric will create unnecessary bulk if you always leave your sweater unbuttoned.

In order to knit this pattern without waist shaping, work in stockinette stitch (k the RS rows, p the WS rows) until the body measures approximately 15.25 (15.25, 15.25, 15.75, **15.75, 16.25, 16.75,** 16.75, 16.75, 16.75) inches [38.5 (38.5, 38.5, 39.5, **39.5, 41, 42,** 42, 42, 42) cm] from the underarm CO or 1.25 inches (3 cm) less than your desired length. Then, work the ribbing as described in the pattern.

If you want wider sleeves but you do not want a wider body:

When choosing your size for this sweater, you may find that you require the body measurements from one size and the sleeve measurements from another. You can easily adjust your sweater to create a wider sleeve.

To modify the circumference of the upper sleeve, you will need to change the length of yoke. First identify the yoke depth of the body size and the sleeve size you wish to knit.

For example, if I want to knit the size 2XL body with size 3XL sleeves, then I would find the yoke depth for both sizes:

- Size 2XL yoke depth is 9 inches (22.5 cm)

- Size 3XL yoke depth is 9.5 inches (24 cm)

You will see that the size 3XL yoke depth is 0.5 inches (1.25 cm) more than the size 2XL yoke depth. You will need to add this amount to your yoke depth in order to increase the circumference of your sleeves.

To do this, you will begin your sweater according to the body size that you intend to knit. For this example, work the Back Shoulders and Back of the Neck Join & Back Yoke sections according to the size 2XL instructions. When you have completed the stockinette portion of the Back Yoke, you will add the necessary length to the yoke depth. In this example, I would add 0.5 inches (1.25 cm) of additional stockinette. You would then continue to work the remaining yoke according to your target body instructions. In this example, the size 2XL.

Next, pick up and knit the Front Yokes according to your target body size until you have completed the Front of the Neck cast on row and the stockinette portions. In this example, I would work the Front Yokes according to the size 2XL, then add the necessary length. Also, I would add 0.5 inches (1.25 cm) of additional stockinette. Complete both Front Yokes and the Body sections according to the target body size. In this example, the size 2XL.

When you reach the Sleeves section, follow all directions according to your target sleeve size. For this example, I would work all instructions according to the size 3XL sleeves.

Little Sock Arms Cardigan

Skill Level: Intermediate

Have you ever let your kiddo or your grandkiddo pick the yarn for their very own sweater? It's the best! Kids really invest in a sweater when they get the chance to plan it. My girls not only share their feelings about the yarn, but they also tend to hang around hopefully whenever I knit, asking "Mom, is it done yet?" When a sweater finally comes off the needles, they help block it too, and have even been known to blow on their sweaters, like a cake full of birthday candles, trying to dry that sweater as quickly as possible. The Little Sock Arms Cardigan is a particularly fun sweater to plan together. With rainbow sleeves, this sweater will light up your kiddo's imagination, and when you are planning a little sweater, there is absolutely nothing better than that! If you are new to sweater knitting, a kiddo sweater is a great place to start. This litte version of the adult Sock Arms Cardigan will give you the chance to try out the construction and techniques used in the grown-up version with faster results.

Construction

This cardigan is knit seamlessly from the top down. The yoke and body are worked first. After completing the body of the sweater, the sleeves are picked up and worked in the round from underarm to wrist, beginning with a sleeve cap shaped using the German Short Rows method (see page 184). The collar is picked up and worked flat. Lastly, the button bands are picked up and worked flat.

Maximum Stitches Used for a Self-Striping Round:
42 (44, 48, 50, **54, 60, 62,** 66, 68, 72)

Sizes

0–6mos (6–12mos, 18mos, 2T, **3T, 4, 6,** 8, 10, 12)

See the Finished Measurements on page 140 to choose your size.

NOTE: Throughout this pattern you will find that **sizes 3T, 4 and 6** appear in bold type. Use this indicator to help you easily find your size as you navigate the pattern.

Yarn

- Sport weight yarn, Must Stash Sport Sock
- (80% superwash merino and 20% nylon, 328 yards / 3.5 ounces [300 m / 100 g])
- Sample shown in "Espalier" (MC, green) and "Ready Player One" (CC, self-striping)
- 1 (1, 1, 1, **2, 2, 2,** 2, 2, 2) skeins of MC and 1 (1, 1, 1, **1, 1, 1,** 1, 1, 2) skeins of CC
- **Main Color:** 210 (240, 275, 325, **390, 450, 500,** 550, 600, 650) yards / [125 (158, 200, 230, **245, 300, 345,** 400, 465, 535) m]
- **Contrasting Color:** 110 (140, 165, 190, **215, 235, 255,** 275, 300, 330) yards / [101 (128, 151, 174, **197, 215, 233,** 252, 275, 302) m]

Yarn Notes

This pattern was knit using a three-ply sport weight yarn to create a dense, warm fabric. Using sport weight yarn at this gauge will give you a snuggly, warm cardigan to keep your little one warm in any weather. If you prefer a lighter fabric, consider using a fingering weight yarn in the same gauge.

Needles

US 4 (3.5 mm) 32-inch (80-cm) circular needles (length as appropriate for your size), or as required to meet gauge

US 3 (3.25 mm) 32-inch (80-cm) circular needles

DPNs or needles for small circumference in the smaller size needles

Gauge

24 stitches and 32 rounds = 4 inches (10 cm) in stockinette stitch on LARGER needles after blocking

Notions

- 6 (6, 6, 7, **7, 8, 9,** 10, 12, 13) [½-inch (1.25-cm)] buttons
- 1 stitch marker
- Scissors
- Tapestry needle
- Scrap yarn
- Tape measure

Finished Measurements

Sample shown is a size 4 with 2 inches (5 cm) of positive ease at the chest. I recommend 2 to 3 inches (5 to 7.5 cm) of ease at the chest for this cardigan.

A. **Chest:** 19 (20, 21, 23, **24, 26, 27,** 29, 31, 33) inches / [47.5 (50, 52.5, 57.5, **60, 65, 67.5,** 72.5, 77.5, 82.5) cm]

B. **Length of Body (Hem to Underarm):** 7 (8, 8.5, 9, **9.5, 10, 11.75,** 13, 14.5, 15.5) inches / [17.5 (20, 21.5, 22.5, **24, 25, 29.5,** 32.5, 36.5, 39) cm]

C. **Sleeve Circumference:** 7 (7.5, 8, 8.5, **9, 10, 10.5,** 11, 11.5, 12) inches / [17.5 (19, 20, 21.5, **22.5, 25, 26.5,** 27.5, 29, 30) cm]

D. **Wrist Circumference:** 5.5 (5.5, 5.75, 5.75, **6, 6, 6.5,** 6.5, 6.75, 6.75) inches / [14 (14, 14.5, 14.5, **15, 15, 16.5,** 16.5, 17, 17) cm]

E. **Sleeve Length:** 7 (8, 8.5, 9, **10, 11, 12,** 13, 14, 15.5) inches / [7.5 (20, 21.5, 22.5, **25, 27.5, 30,** 32.5, 35, 39) cm]

F. **Yoke Depth:** 3.75 (4.25, 4.25, 4.5, **4.75, 5, 5.25,** 5.75, 6, 6.25) inches / [9.5 (10.5, 10.5, 11.5, **12, 12.5, 13,** 14.5, 15, 15.5) cm]

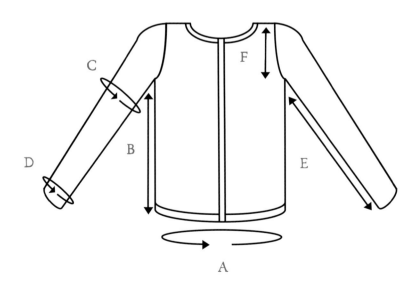

Abbreviations	
BO	bind off
BOR	beginning of round
CC	contrasting color
CO	cast on
dec	decrease
DPNs	double pointed needles
DS	double stitch
inc	increase
k	knit
k2tog	knit two together
m	marker
MC	main color
m1L	make one left
m1R	make one right
p	purl
pm	place marker
rep	repeat
RH	right-hand
RS	right side
sl	slip
sl1k	slip one knitwise
sl1p	slip one purlwise
ssk	slip, slip, knit
st(s)	stitch(es)
WS	wrong side
wyib	with yarn in back
wyif	with yarn in front

Pattern

Back Right Shoulder

Using LARGER needles and MC, CO 6 (6, 8, 8, **10, 12, 14**, 14, 16, 18) sts.

Row 1 (RS): K all.

Row 2 (WS): P all.

In this section, you will be casting on sts for the back of the neck. Use the Cable cast on for these CO sts. For a tutorial on the Cable cast on, see page 177.

Row 3 (RS): CO3, k to end. [3 sts inc]

Row 4 (WS): P all.

Rep Rows 3 and 4 until you have 12 (12, 14, 17, **19, 21, 23**, 26, 28, 30) sts on your needles. End on a WS row. Break yarn, leaving a 6-inch (15-cm) tail. Place sts on hold.

Back Left Shoulder

Using LARGER needles and MC, CO 6 (6, 8, 8, **10, 12, 14**, 14, 16, 18) sts.

Row 1 (RS): K all.

Row 2 (WS): P all.

Row 3 (RS): K all.

Row 4 (WS): CO3, p to end. [3 sts inc]

Row 5 (RS): K all.

Rep Rows 4 and 5 until you have 12 (12, 14, 17, **19, 21, 23**, 26, 28, 30) sts on your needles. End after completing a WS row. Do not break yarn.

Back of the Neck Join & Back Yoke

Joining Row (RS): K to end, CO 19 (22, 21, 19, **16, 18**, **15**, 13, 13, 15) sts. Place the Back Right Shoulder on your needle with the RS facing you. K to end. [19 (22, 21, 19, **16**, **18, 15**, 13, 13, 15) sts inc; 43 (46, 49, 53, **54, 60, 61**, 65, 69, 75) sts total]

Work in stockinette stitch (k the RS rows, p the WS rows). End after completing a WS row. Your Back Yoke should measure approximately 2.75 (3.25, 3, 3.5, **3, 3.5, 3,** 3.5, 3.5, 3.75) inches [7 (8, 7.5, 9, **7.5, 9, 7.5,** 9, 9, 9.5) cm] from the top of the shoulder CO. You will now begin increasing along the underarms.

Row 1 (RS): K1, m1R, k to last st, m1L, k1. [2 sts inc]

Row 2 (WS): P all.

Row 3 (RS): K all.

Row 4 (WS): P all.

Rep Rows 1–4 until you have 47 (50, 53, 57, **58, 64, 67,** 71, 75, 81) sts. End after completing Row 4.

Row 5 (RS): K1, m1R, k to last st, m1L, k1. [2 sts inc]

Row 6 (WS): P all.

Rep Rows 5 and 6 until you have 53 (56, 59, 63, **66, 72, 75,** 79, 85, 91) sts. End after completing a WS row. Break yarn, leaving a 6-inch (15-cm) tail.

Place your Back Yoke sts on a piece of scrap yarn.

Front Right Yoke

Start at the shoulder edge. With the RS facing you and using LARGER needles and MC, pick up and knit 6 (6, 8, 8, **10, 12, 14,** 14, 16, 18) sts along the Back Right Shoulder CO edge.

> Note: When picking up sts along the CO edge, pick up the Front Shoulder sts directly into the Back Shoulder CO sts, not in between.

Work 5 (7, 7, 5, **7, 7, 7,** 9, 9, 9) rows in stockinette stitch (k the RS rows, p the WS rows). End after completing a WS row. You will now begin increasing along the neckline.

Row 1 (RS): K to last st, m1R, k1. [1 st inc]

Row 2 (WS): P all.

Rep Rows 1 and 2 until you have 10 (12, 13, 15, **15, 16, 16,** 18, 20, 21) sts on your needles. End after completing a WS row.

Row 3 (RS): K to last st, m1R, k1. [1 st inc]

Row 4 (WS): P1, m1R purlwise, p to end. [1 st inc]

Rep Rows 3 and 4 until you have 15 (17, 18, 20, **20, 23, 23,** 25, 27, 30) sts. End after completing a RS row.

Front of the Neck CO Row (WS): CO 6 (5, 5, 5, **5, 5, 5,** 5, 5, 5) sts, p to end. [6 (5, 5, 5, **5, 5, 5,** 5, 5, 5) sts inc; 21 (22, 23, 25, **25, 28, 28,** 30, 32, 35) sts total]

Work in stockinette stitch (k the RS rows, p the WS rows) until the Front Right Yoke measures 2.75 (3.25, 3, 3.5, **3, 3.5, 3,** 3.5, 3.5, 3.75) inches [7 (8, 7.5, 9, **7.5, 9, 7.5,** 9, 9, 9.5) cm] from the top of the shoulder. End after completing a WS row. You will now begin increasing along the underarm.

Row 5 (RS): K1, m1R, k to end. [1 st inc]

Row 6 (WS): P all.

Row 7 (RS): K all.

Row 8 (WS): P all.

Work Rows 5–8 until you have 22 (23, 24, 26, **27, 30, 31,** 33, 35, 38) sts. End after completing Row 8.

Row 9 (RS): K1, m1R, k to end. [1 st inc]

Row 10 (WS): P all.

Rep Rows 9 and 10 until you have 24 (26, 27, 29, **31, 34, 35,** 37, 40, 43) sts. End after completing a WS Row. Break yarn, leaving a 6-inch (15-cm) tail.

Place your Front Right Yoke sts on a piece of scrap yarn.

Front Left Yoke

Start at the neckline edge. With the RS facing you and using LARGER needles and MC, pick up and knit 6 (6, 8, 8, **10, 12, 14**, 14, 16, 18) sts along the Back Left Shoulder CO edge.

Work 5 (7, 7, 5, **7, 7, 7**, 9, 9, 9) rows in stockinette stitch (k the RS rows, p the WS rows). End after completing a WS row. You will now begin increasing along the neckline.

Row 1 (RS): K1, m1L, k to end. [1 st inc]

Row 2 (WS): P all.

Rep Rows 1 and 2 until you have 10 (12, 13, 15, **15, 16, 16**, 18, 20, 21) sts on your needles. End after completing a RS row.

Next Row (WS): P to last st, m1L purlwise, p1. [1 st inc]

Row 3 (RS): K1, m1L, k to end. [1 st inc]

Row 4 (WS): P to last st, m1L purlwise, p1. [1 st inc]

Rep Rows 3 and 4 until you have 15 (17, 18, 20, **20, 23, 23**, 25, 27, 30) sts. End after completing a WS row.

Front of the Neck CO Row (WS): P to end, CO 6 (5, 5, 5, **5, 5, 5**, 5, 5, 5) sts. [6 (5, 5, 5, **5, 5, 5**, 5, 5, 5) sts inc; 21 (22, 23, 25, **25, 28, 28**, 30, 32, 35) sts total]

Work in stockinette stitch (k the RS rows, p the WS rows) until the Front Right Yoke measures 2.75 (3.25, 3, 3.5, **3, 3.5, 3**, 3.5, 3.5, 3.75) inches [7 (8, 7.5, 9, **7.5, 9, 7.5**, 9, 9, 9.5) cm] from the top of the shoulder. End after completing a WS row. You will now begin increasing along the underarm.

Row 5 (RS): K to last st, m1L, k1. [1 st inc]

Row 6 (WS): P all.

Row 7 (RS): K all.

Row 8 (WS): P all.

Work Rows 5–8 until you have 22 (23, 24, 26, **27, 30, 31**, 33, 35, 38) sts. End after completing Row 8.

Row 9 (RS): K to last st, m1L, k1. [1 st inc]

Row 10 (WS): P.

Rep Rows 9 and 10 until you have 24 (26, 27, 29, **31, 34, 35,** 37, 40, 43) sts. End after completing a WS Row.

Joining the Front & Back Yokes

Joining Row (RS): K across 24 (26, 27, 29, **31, 34, 35,** 37, 40, 43) Front Left Yoke sts, CO 4 (4, 4, 6, **6, 6, 6**, 8, 8, 8) underarm sts, k across 53 (56, 59, 63, **66, 72, 75**, 79, 85, 91) Back Yoke sts, CO 4 (4, 4, 6, **6, 6, 6**, 8, 8, 8) underarm sts, k across 24 (26, 27, 29, **31, 34, 35,** 37, 40, 43) Front Right Yoke sts.

You should now have 109 (116, 121, 133, **140, 152, 157,** 169, 181, 193) sts on your needles.

Body

Work in stockinette stitch (k the RS rows, p the WS rows) until your work measures approximately 6 (7, 7.5, 8, **8.5, 9, 10.75,** 12, 13.5, 14.5) inches [15 (17.5, 19, 20, **21.5, 22.5, 27,** 30, 34, 36.5) cm] from the underarm CO. End after completing a WS row. If you would like to add length to your sweater, do so here.

Change to SMALLER needles.

Work 1x1 ribbing (k1, p1) until the Body measures approximately 7 (8, 8.5, 9, **9.5, 10, 11.75,** 13, 14.5, 15.5) inches [17.5 (20, 21.5, 22.5, **24, 25, 29.5,** 32.5, 36.5, 39) cm] from the underarm or your desired length. End after completing a WS row. BO all sts in pattern. Break yarn, leaving a 6-inch (15-cm) tail.

Sleeves (both worked identically)

> Note: Seamless set-in sleeves are new to many knitters. When working a set-in sleeve, you may notice that the Anchor Round looks loose after completing the sleeve cap. This is not an error in knitting or in the pattern. This round tends to loosen naturally as you work the short rows for the sleeve cap. To get a clean sleeve cap, see the "Perfecting the Set-In Sleeve" section on page 146 after you complete your sleeves.

Using MC and LARGER needles for small circumference knitting, pick up 42 (44, 48, 50, **54, 60, 62,** 66, 68, 72) sts around the armhole, as follows:

Anchor Round: Pick up and knit 21 (22, 24, 25, **27, 30, 31,** 33, 34, 36) sts evenly between the middle of the underarm and the shoulder seam. Pick up and knit 21 (22, 24, 25, **27, 30, 31,** 33, 34, 36) sts evenly between the shoulder seam and the middle of the underarm. Place a BOR marker. Break MC, leaving a 6-inch (15-cm) tail. Place a removable marker after stitch 7 (7, 8, 8, **9, 10, 10,** 11, 11, 12). Place another removable marker after stitch 35 (37, 40, 42, **45, 50, 52,** 55, 57, 60). You should have 28 (30, 32, 34, **36, 40, 42,** 44, 46, 48) sts between the 2 removable markers.

You will now begin short row shaping the sleeve cap.

Row 1 (RS): Sl15 (15, 17, 17, **19, 21, 22,** 24, 24, 26) purlwise, join CC, k13 (15, 15, 17, **17, 19, 19,** 19, 21, 21), turn work.

Row 2 (WS): DS, p13 (15, 15, 17, **17, 19, 19,** 19, 21, 21), turn work.

Row 3 (RS): DS, k to last DS, resolve DS, k1, turn work.

Row 4 (WS): DS, p to last DS, resolve DS, p1, turn work.

Work Rows 3 and 4 until the last st next to the second removable marker has been worked as a DS. In the following row, you will work a DS on the last st next to the first removable marker.

Next Row (RS): DS, knit to the beginning of the row, resolving all DS sts as you come to them. There will be one remaining DS to resolve on the next round. Remove the removable markers ONLY. Leave the BOR marker in place.

You will now begin working in the round. Knit six rounds.

Sleeve Decrease Round: K1, k2tog, k to last 3 sts, ssk, k1. [2 sts dec]

Knit 6 (6, 6, 5, **5, 4, 4,** 4, 4, 4) rounds.

Rep the previous 7 (7, 7, 6, **6, 5, 5,** 5, 5, 5) rounds until you have 32 (32, 34, 34, **36, 36, 38,** 38, 40, 40) sts.

Work in stockinette stitch (k every round) until the sleeve measures 5.5 (6.5, 7, 7.5, **8.5, 9, 10,** 11, 12, 13.5) inches [14 (16.5, 17.5, 19, **21.5, 22.5, 25,** 27.5, 30, 34) cm] from the underarm or 1.5 (1.5, 1.5, 1.5, **1.5, 2, 2,** 2, 2, 2) inches [4 (4, 4, 4, **4, 5, 5,** 5, 5, 5) cm] less than your desired length.

> Note: When using a self-striping yarn, knit one complete round of a new color before starting the ribbing.

Change to SMALLER needles. Work 1x1 ribbing (k1, p1) until ribbing measures 1.5 (1.5, 1.5, 1.5, **1.5, 2, 2,** 2, 2, 2) inches [4 (4, 4, 4, **4, 5, 5,** 5, 5, 5) cm], or desired length.

Note: When using a self-striping yarn, on the first round of each new color, knit all the purl sts in that round. Substituting a knit st for a purl st in the color change rounds will give you a clean color transition. When you have completed the first round of the new color, continue to work the purl sts according to the pattern.

Note: If your self-striping yardage is limited, consider shortening the sleeves or using the MC for your sleeve cuffs.

BO all sts in pattern and break yarn, leaving a 6-inch (15-cm) tail.

Collar

Begin with the RS facing you. With SMALLER needles and MC, pick up and knit 6 (5, 5, 5, **5, 5, 5,** 5, 5, 5) sts along the front right CO edge of the neckline, 3 of 4 sts along the slope of the neck, all sts along the back of across the back of the neck, 3 of 4 sts along the slope of the neck and 6 (5, 5, 5, **5, 5, 5,** 5, 5, 5) sts along the front left CO edge of the neckline. You will need an odd number of sts on your needles.

Ribbing Row (WS): (P1, k1) rep to last st, p1.

Ribbing Row (RS): (K1, p1) rep to last st, k1.

Work 1x1 ribbing for three rows. End after completing a WS row. BO all sts in pattern. Break yarn, leaving a 6-inch (15-cm) tail.

Right Front Edge Button Band (Buttonhole Side)

Begin at the hem with the RS facing you. With SMALLER needles and MC, pick up and knit 53 (57, 61, 69, **71, 75, 89,** 99, 109, 117) sts, ending on an odd number.

Note: You will be picking up approximately 3 of 4 sts. You may need to make minor adjustments to this ratio in order to pick up the appropriate number of sts. If you feel that you need to pick up significantly more sts than listed, I suggest that you choose a larger size and work the buttonhole instructions according to that size.

Ribbing Row (WS): Sl1p wyif, (k1, p1) rep to end.

Ribbing Row (RS): Sl1k wyib, (p1, k1) rep to end.

Work 1x1 ribbing for three rows. End after completing a WS row.

In the following two rows, you will work in pattern (knitting the knit sts and purling the purl sts). You will be binding off sts to create a buttonhole. Binding off sts will leave a st on your RH needle. Leave this stitch on your RH needle, then continue to work in pattern.

Buttonhole Row (RS): Work 3 (5, 4, 3, **4, 5, 3,** 3, 4, 3) sts in pattern, [BO 2, work 6 (6, 7, 7, **7, 6, 7,** 7, 6, 6) sts in pattern] 5 (5, 5, 6, **6, 7, 8,** 9, 11, 12) times, BO 2, work in pattern to end.

Buttonhole Row (WS): Work 3 (5, 5, 4, **5, 5, 4,** 4, 4, 4) sts in pattern, [CO 2 at the buttonhole gap, work 7 (7, 8, 8, **8, 7, 8,** 8, 7, 7) sts in pattern] 5 (5, 5, 6, **6, 7, 8,** 9, 11, 12) times, CO 2 at the buttonhole gap, work in pattern to end.

Work 1x1 ribbing for two rows. End after completing a WS row. BO all sts in pattern. Break yarn, leaving a 6-inch (15-cm) tail.

Left Front Edge Button Band (Button Side)

Begin at the neckline with the RS facing you. With SMALLER needles and MC, pick up and knit 53 (57, 61, 69, **71, 75, 89,** 99, 109, 117) sts, ending on an odd number.

> **Note:** You will be picking up approximately 3 of 4 sts. If you picked up an alternative number of stitches for the Right Front Edge Button Band, pick up the same number of sts for this button band.

Ribbing Row (WS): Sl1p wyif, (k1, p1) rep to end.

Ribbing Row (RS): Sl1k wyib, (p1, k1) rep to end.

Work 1x1 ribbing for a total of seven rows. End after completing a WS row. BO all sts in pattern. Break yarn, leaving a 6-inch (15-cm) tail.

Finishing

Attach 6 (6, 6, 7, **7, 8, 9,** 10, 12, 13) [½-inch (1.25-cm)] buttons in alignment with the buttonholes. Weave in all ends. For the best results, be sure to wet block your finished sweater. Soak the sweater in cold water, squeezing to remove air bubbles. Squeeze out the water, but do not wring. Roll the sweater in a dry towel, burrito-style, and press on it to remove excess water. Lay the sweater flat to dry, using a measuring tape to be sure it is laid out with the correct dimensions.

Perfecting the Set-In Sleeve

AFTER knitting your sweater and BEFORE weaving in ends, locate the Anchor Round of your sleeve. This round will be knit in the MC and should be easy to spot. If the sts in the Anchor Round look loose, tighten them. You will tighten one half of the sts first and then the other half. Do this by starting at the shoulder seam and working your way down toward the underarm. First, locate the Anchor Round (Photo 1). Using a tapestry needle, locate the left and right leg of each loose stitch (Photo 2). Carefully, pull the right leg of the st to tighten the left side of the st. This will create a long, loose loop (Photo 3). Pull the left leg of the next st (one st closer to the underarm) to tighten this loop. Then pull the right leg to tighten the left leg.

Continue to work in this manner until you reach the center of the underarm. Turn your pullover inside out and pull the tail of the Anchor Round to tighten the final loose loop. Repeat this process for the second half of the Anchor Round.

Showered in Rainbows Baby Sweater

Skill Level: Intermediate

When I get a baby shower invitation, my first thought is: It's time to knit a baby sweater! Baby sweaters have two major advantages when you are knitting with self-striping yarn. First, they are little. Little sweaters mean that every row has fewer stitches. That is great for self-striping yarn, especially if your yarn has narrow stripes. More importantly, this sweater requires so little yardage! The Showered in Rainbows Baby Sweater gives you the chance to knit an entire garment with just one skein of yarn. ONE. SKEIN. Time to shower that baby in rainbows!

Construction

This sweater is knit flat. The two side panels are knit first. Then the back is knit from the edge of each side panel in two separate sections and connected using a three-needle bind off. Next, the fronts are picked up and knit from the side panel edge to the button bands. The sleeves are worked in the round from the underarm to the cuff. Finally, the bottom border and neckline are worked last. For a detailed schematic of the construction of the body of this sweater, see Fig. 1.

Three-needle bind off shown in RED.
Arrows indicate directions of knitting.

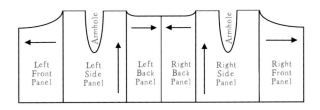

1

Sizes

Newborn (0–3mos, 3–6mos, **6–12mos, 18mos, 2T**)

NOTE: Throughout this pattern you will find that **sizes 6–12mos, 18mos and 2T** appear in bold type. Use this indicator to help you easily find your size as you navigate the pattern. See the Finished Measurements on page 149 to choose your size.

Maximum Sitches Used for a Self-Striping Row: 106 (112, 118, **124, 130, 142**)

Yarn

- Fingering weight yarn, Kirby Wirby Soft & Squishy
- (75% superwash merino and 25% nylon, 440 yards / 3.5 ounces [402 m / 100 g])
- Sample shown in "Blurple"
- 1 skein
- 240 (280, 320, **360, 400, 440**) yards / [220 (256, 293, **330, 366, 403**) m]

Yarn Notes

When I knit a baby sweater, I like to keep the fabric light. Fingering weight sweaters are perfect for layering over a baby onesie. I like to knit with a superwash merino sock yarn so the sweater is soft and easy to clean.

Needles

US 4 (3.5 mm) 32-inch (80-cm) circular needles (length as appropriate for your size), or as required to meet gauge

US 2 (3.25 mm) 32-inch (80-cm) circular needles

DPNs or needles for small circumference in the smaller size needles

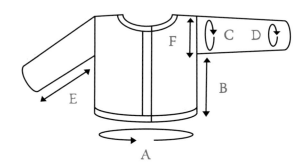

Gauge

24 stitches and 32 rounds = 4 inches (10 cm) in stockinette stitch on LARGER needles after blocking

Notions

- 3 [½-inch (1.25-cm)] buttons
- 1 stitch marker
- Scissors
- Tapestry needle
- Scrap yarn
- Tape measure

Abbreviations	
BO	bind off
BOR	beginning of round
CO	cast on
dec	decrease
DPNs	double pointed needles
k	knit
k2tog	knit two together
m	marker
p	purl
p2tog	purl two together
rep	repeat
RH	right-hand
RS	right side
sl	slip
sl1p	slip one purlwise
ssk	slip, slip, knit
ssp	slip, slip, purl
st(s)	stitch(es)
WS	wrong side
w&t	wrap and turn
wyif	with yarn in front

Finished Measurements

Sample shown is a size 0–3mos. I recommend 1 to 2 inches (2.5 to 5 cm) of ease at the chest for this cardigan.

A. **Chest:** 17 (18.25, 19.25, **20.25, 21, 23.25**) inches / [42.5 (45.5, 48, **50.5, 52.5, 58**) cm]

B. **Length of Body (Hem to Underarm):** 4 (5, 5.75, **6.5, 7.25, 8**) inches / [10 (12.5, 14.5, **16.5, 18, 20**) cm]

C. **Sleeve Circumference:** 6 (6.5, 7, **7.5, 8, 8.5**) inches / [15 (16.5, 17.5, **19, 20.5, 21.5**) cm]

D. **Wrist Circumference:** 5 (5.5, 6, **6.5, 7, 7.5**) inches / [12.5 (14, 15, **16.5, 17.5, 19**) cm]

E. **Sleeve Length:** 6 (6.5, 7, **8, 8.5, 9**) inches / [15 (16.5, 17.5, **20, 21.5, 22.5**) cm]

F. **Yoke Depth:** 3 (3.25, 3.5, **3.75, 4, 4.25**) inches / [7.5 (8, 9, **9.5, 10, 10.5**) cm]

Pattern

Side Panels

Using LARGER needles, CO 24 (28, 32, **34, 36, 40**) sts. Work in stockinette stitch (k the RS rows, p the WS rows) until your work measures 3 (4, 4.75, **5.5, 6.25, 7**) inches [7.5 (10, 12, **14, 15.5, 17.5**) cm] from the CO edge. End after completing a WS row.

Underarm Division Row (RS): K12 (14, 16, **17, 18, 20**) sts. Place the next 12 (14, 16, **17, 18, 20**) sts onto a piece of scrap yarn.

Work in stockinette stitch until your work measures 3 (3.25, 3.5, **3.75, 4, 4.25**) inches [7.5 (8, 9, **9.5, 10, 10.5**) cm] from the Underarm Division. End after completing a WS row.

You will now begin short row shaping the shoulder.

Row 1 (RS): K to 4 sts before the end, w&t.

Row 2 (WS): P all.

Row 3 (RS): K to 4 sts before last wrapped st, w&t.

Row 4 (WS): P all.

Rep Rows 3 and 4 an additional - (-, -, **1, 1, 1**) time. End after completing a WS row.

> **Note:** See page 184 for information on how to work Wrap & Turn Short Rows.

Next Row (RS): K all, working wraps together with wrapped sts as you come to them.

Next Row (WS): P all.

Break yarn, leaving a 6-inch (15-cm) tail. Place these sts onto a piece of scrap yarn.

Place the 12 (14, 16, **17, 18, 20**) sts held at the underarm on your LARGER needles. Beginning on a RS row, join yarn and work in stockinette stitch until your work measures 3 (3.25, 3.5, **3.75, 4, 4.25**) inches [7.5 (8, 9, **9.5, 10, 10.5**) cm] from the Underarm Division. End after completing a WS row.

You will now begin short row shaping the shoulder.

Row 5 (RS): K all.

Row 6 (WS): P to last 4 sts, w&t.

Row 7 (RS): K all.

Row 8 (WS): P to 4 sts before last wrapped st, w&t.

Rep Rows 7 and 8 an additional - (-, -, **1, 1, 1**) time. End after completing a WS row.

Next Row (RS): K all.

Next Row (WS): P all, working wraps together with wrapped sts as you come to them.

Place the held sts onto your needles. Align the two sets of 12 (14, 16, **17, 18, 20**) sts. With the RS of the work facing each other and the WS of the work facing out, use a third needle and work the three-needle bind off (see page 180). Break yarn, leaving a 6-inch (15-cm) tail.

Repeat this section to create the second Side Panel.

Right Back Panel

> **Note:** The Right Back Panel refers to the RH side of the cardigan as worn. That is, when your cardigan is complete, this panel will be on the right side of the body. All references to "right" and "left" throughout the pattern will be "as worn."

Before working the Right Back Panel, choose one of your Side Panels and mark it as the Right Side Panel. Before working this section, the Side Panels are identical, so it does not matter which Side Panel you choose. Once you begin this section, it will be important that you do not confuse the two.

Use LARGER needles with the RS facing you. Beginning at the shoulder seam of your Right Side Panel, pick up and knit 43 (51, 57, **65, 69, 75**) sts along the edge of the Side Panel. You will be picking up approximately 3 sts for every four rows.

Next Row (WS): P all.

Row 1 (RS): K1, ssk, k to end. [1 st dec]

Row 2 (WS): P all.

Rep Rows 1 and 2 an additional two times. End after completing a WS row [40 (48, 54, **62, 66, 72**) sts]. Work in stockinette stitch until your work measures approximately 2.25 (2.25, 2, **2.25, 2.25, 2.5**) inches [5.5 (5.5, 5, **5.5, 5.5, 6.5**) cm] from the Side Panel edge. Place sts onto a piece of scrap yarn. Break yarn, leaving a 6-inch (15-cm) tail.

Left Back Panel

Use LARGER needles with the RS facing you. Beginning at the bottom corner of your Left Side Panel, pick up and knit 43 (51, 57, **65, 69, 75**) sts along the edge of the Side Panel. You will be picking up approximately 3 sts for every four rows.

Next Row (WS): P all.

Row 1 (RS): K to last 3 sts, k2tog, k1. [1 st dec]

Row 2 (WS): P all.

Rep Rows 1 and 2 an additional two times. End after completing a WS row [40 (48, 54, **62, 66, 72**) sts]. Work in stockinette stitch until your work measures approximately 2.25 (2.25, 2, **2.25, 2.25, 2.5**) inches [5.5 (5.5, 5, **5.5, 5.5, 6.5**) cm] from the Side Panel edge.

Joining the Back Panels

Place the held Back Right Panel sts onto your needles. Align the two sets of 40 (48, 54, **62, 66, 72**) sts. With the WS of the panels facing each other and the RS of the panels facing out, use a third needle and work the three-needle bind off (see page 180). Break yarn, leaving a 6-inch (15-cm) tail.

Right Front Panel

Use LARGER needles with the RS facing you. Beginning at the bottom corner of your Right Side Panel, pick up and knit 43 (51, 57, **65, 69, 75**) sts along the edge of your Side Panel. You will end at the shoulder seam created by the three-needle bind off. You will be picking up approximately 3 sts for every four rows.

In the following row, you will be binding off sts to create a buttonhole. Binding off sts will leave a st on your RH needle. Leave this stitch on your RH needle and continue to work the row as instructed.

Buttonhole Row (RS): Knit 16 (22, 28, **36, 40, 45**), (BO 2, k4) 2 times, BO 2, k2.

Buttonhole Row (WS): K3, (CO 2 at the buttonhole gap, k5) 2 times, CO 2 at the buttonhole gap, k to end.

Knit three rows. End after completing a RS row. BO all sts knitwise on a WS row. Break yarn, leaving a 6-inch (15-cm) tail.

Left Front Panel

Use LARGER needles with the RS facing you. Beginning at the shoulder seam of your Left Side Panel, pick up and knit 43 (51, 57, **65, 69, 75**) sts along the edge of the Side Panel. You will be picking up approximately 3 sts for every four rows.

Next Row (WS): P all.

Row 1 (RS): K1, ssk, k to end. [1 st dec]

Row 2 (WS): P to last 3 sts, ssp, p1. [1 st dec]

Rep Rows 1 and 2 an additional 2 (3, 3, **3, 3, 3**) times. End after completing a WS row. [37 (43, 49, **57, 61, 67**) sts]

Row 3 (RS): K1, ssk, k to end. [1 st dec]

Row 4 (WS): P all.

Rep Rows 3 and 4 an additional 1 (1, 1, **1, 1, 2**) time(s). End after completing a WS row. [35 (41, 47, **55, 59, 64**) sts]

Work in stockinette stitch until your work measures approximately 1.75 (1.75, 1.75, **1.75, 1.75, 2**) inches [4.5 (4.5, 4.5, **4.5, 4.5, 5**) cm] from the Side Panel edge. End after completing a RS row.

Beginning on a WS row, knit eight rows. End after completing a RS row. BO all sts knitwise on a WS row. Break yarn, leaving a 6-inch (15-cm) tail.

Next Row (WS): P all.

Row 1 (RS): K to last 3 sts, k2tog, k1. [1 st dec]

Row 2 (WS): P1, p2tog, p to end. [1 st dec]

Rep Rows 1 and 2 an additional 2 (3, 3, **3, 3, 3**) times. End after completing a WS row. [37 (43, 49, **57, 61, 67**) sts]

Row 3 (RS): K to last 3 sts, k2tog, k1. [1 st dec]

Row 4 (WS): P all.

Rep Rows 3 and 4 an additional 1 (1, 1, **1, 1, 2**) time(s). End after completing a WS row. [35 (41, 47, **55, 59, 64**) sts]

Work in stockinette stitch until your work measures approximately 1.75 (1.75, 1.75, **1.75, 1.75, 2**) inches [4.5 (4.5, 4.5, **4.5, 4.5, 5**) cm] from the Side Panel edge. End after completing a RS row.

You will now begin working the Button Band.

Beginning on a WS row, knit three rows. End after completing a WS row.

Sleeves (both worked identically)

Using LARGER needles for small circumference knitting, pick up 36 (40, 42, **44, 48, 50**) sts around the armhole opening. You will be picking up approximately 3 sts for every four rows. Place a BOR marker and join to work in the round.

Knit eight rounds.

Sleeve Decrease Round: K1, k2tog, k to last 3 sts, ssk, k1. [2 sts dec]

Knit 9 (10, 12, **14, 16, 17**) rounds.

Rep the previous 10 (11, 13, **15, 17, 18**) rounds (including Sleeve Decrease Round) until you have 30 (34, 36, **38, 42, 44**) sts.

Work in stockinette stitch (k every round) until the sleeve measures 5.25 (5.75, 6.25, **7.25, 7.75, 8.25**) inches [13.5 (14.5, 16, **18.5, 19.5, 21**) cm] from the underarm or 0.75 inches (2 cm) less than your desired length.

Change to SMALLER needles.

Work 1x1 ribbing (k1, p1) until cuff measures approximately 0.75 inches (2 cm) or desired length. BO all sts in pattern. Break yarn, leaving a 6-inch (15-cm) tail.

Bottom Border

Use LARGER needles with the RS facing you. Begin at the lower edge of the Front Left Panel. Pick up and knit 106 (112, 118, **124, 130, 142**) sts evenly along the entire lower edge of the cardigan.

Note: Feel free to make adjustments to the number of sts you pick up for the bottom border. The precise number of sts you pick up for the bottom border is not critical.

Bottom Border Row (RS and WS): Sl1p wyif, k to end.

Work the Bottom Border Row an additional seven times. End after completing a RS row. BO all sts knitwise on a WS row. Break yarn, leaving a 6-inch (15-cm) tail.

Neckline Border

Begin with the RS facing you. With LARGER needles, pick up and knit 4 sts along the front right buttonband edge, 3 of every 4 sts along the slope of the neck on the Right Front Panel, 3 of every 4 sts along the Back Panels, 3 of every 4 sts along the slope of the neck Left Front Panel, and 4 sts along the front left button band edge.

Neckline Row (RS and WS): Sl1p wyif, k to end.

Work the Neckline Row an additional three times. End after completing a RS row. BO all sts knitwise on a WS row. Break yarn, leaving a 6-inch (15-cm) tail.

Finishing

Attach 3 [½-inch (1.25-cm)] buttons in alignment with the buttonholes. Weave in all ends. For the best results, be sure to wet block your finished sweater. Soak the sweater in cold water, squeezing to remove air bubbles. Squeeze out the water, but do not wring. Roll the sweater in a dry towel, burrito-style, and press on it to remove excess water. Lay the sweater flat to dry, using a measuring tape to be sure it is laid out with the correct dimensions.

Bright Axis Tee
Skill Level: Intermediate

There is practically nothing I love more than knitting in stockinette stitch. These days, when I am packing up my project bag for long car rides or the kids' activities, I don't reach for socks—I grab a sweater. Stockinette sweaters are knitting heaven, especially when there is a rainbow at the end of the stockinette tunnel. And by tunnel, I obviously mean the body of my sweater. This sweater plays with the traditional drop shoulder construction by turning the yoke on its axis. Flattering vertical stripes stretch from shoulder to shoulder in this casual summer tee. Even though this little sweater has huge impact, there isn't a single complicated stitch in the entire pattern. Knitting bonus: This tee can be easily customized by using the "Getting the Right Fit" section on page 160. Perfect for long color sequences and dramatic color changes, this tee will be the project you want to grab every time you head out the door.

Construction

The body of this sweater is knit in the round from the bottom up. After working the body, the back yoke is worked flat using the German Short Rows method (see page 184). Next, the back border is worked vertically as an attached border. The front yoke and front border are worked identically to the back yoke and back border. The shoulders are joined using the Mattress Stitch seaming method (see page 183) to add structure to the tee. Finally, the ribbed border is picked up and worked around the opening of the armholes.

Maximum Stitches Used for a Self-Striping Row:
33 (35, 36, 39, **41, 45, 50, 54,** 57, 61, 66)

Sizes

XS (S, M, L, **XL, 2XL, 3XL, 4XL,** 5XL, 6XL, 7XL)

See the Finished Measurements on page 156 to choose your size.

NOTE: Throughout this pattern you will find that **sizes XL, 2XL, 3XL and 4XL** appear in bold type. Use this indicator to help you easily find your size as you navigate the pattern.

Yarn

- Fingering weight yarn, Must Stash Perfect Sock
- (75% superwash merino and 25% nylon, 440 yards / 3.5 ounces [402 m / 100 g])
- Sample shown in "Charcoal" (MC) and "Kama" (CC)
- 2 (2, 2, 2, **2, 2, 2, 3,** 3, 3, 3) skeins of MC and 1 (1, 1, 2, **2, 2, 2, 2,** 2, 2, 2) skeins of CC
- **Main Color:** 525 (575, 620, 690, **790, 840, 880, 930,** 975, 1015, 1060) yards / [480 (525, 567, 630, **722, 768, 805, 850,** 892, 928, 970) m]
- **Contrasting Color:** 310 (360, 410, 460, **510, 600, 675, 740,** 800, 875, 960) yards / [284 (329, 375, 421, **466, 549, 617, 677,** 732, 800, 878) m]

Yarn Notes

This pattern was knit using a three-ply fingering weight yarn. Three-ply yarn has wonderful drape and sturdy structure. Using fingering weight yarn will make this tee light and airy. If you prefer a denser fabric, consider using a sport weight yarn.

Needles

US 5 (3.75 mm) 32-inch (80-cm) circular needles (length as appropriate for your size), or as required to meet gauge

US 3 (3.25 mm) 32-inch (80-cm) circular needles (length as appropriate for your size), or as required to meet gauge

DPNs or needles for small circumference in the smaller size needles

Gauge

24 stitches and 32 rounds = 4 inches (10 cm) in stockinette stitch on LARGER needles after blocking

Notions

- 2 stitch markers
- Scissors
- Tapestry needle
- Scrap yarn
- Tape measure

Finished Measurements

Sample shown is a size XL with 12 inches (30 cm) of positive ease at the bust. I recommend 4 to 12 inches (10 to 30 cm) of ease at the bust for this tee.

A. **Bust:** 32 (36, 40, 44, **48, 52, 56, 60,** 64, 68, 72) inches / [80 (90, 100, 110, **120, 130, 140, 150,** 160, 170, 180) cm]

B. **Length of Body (Hem to Underarm):** 12 (11.5, 11.25, 10.75, **10.5, 9.75, 9, 8.75,** 8, 7.5, 7) inches / [30 (29, 28.5, 27, **26.5, 24.5, 22.5, 22,** 20, 19, 17.5) cm]

C. **Sleeve Circumference:** 11 (11.75, 12, 13, **13.75, 15, 16, 17,** 18, 19, 20) inches / [27.5 (29, 30, 32.5, **34.5, 37.5, 40, 42.5,** 45, 47.5, 50) cm]

D. **Yoke Depth:** 7.25 (7.75, 8, 8.75, **9, 10, 10.75, 11.5,** 12.25, 13, 13.75) inches / [18 (19.5, 20, 22, **22.5, 25, 27, 29,** 31, 32.5, 34.5) cm]

E. **Neckline (Unstretched, Flat):** 11 (11, 11, 11, **12, 12, 12.5, 12.5,** 13, 13, 13) inches / [27.5 (27.5, 27.5, 27.5, **30, 30, 31.5, 31.5,** 32.5, 32.5, 32.5) cm]

F. **Shoulder Seam:** 6.75 (8.25, 9.75, 11.25, **12.25, 13.75, 15, 16.50,** 17.75, 19.25, 20.75) inches / [17 (20.5, 24.5, 28, **30.5, 34.5, 37.5, 41.5,** 44.5, 48, 52) cm]

G. **Total Length:** 20.25 (20.75, 21, 21.75, **22, 23, 24, 25,** 25.75, 26.75, 27.75) inches / [42.5 (43.25, 43.5, 44.5, **45, 46.5, 48, 49,** 50, 52, 53) cm]

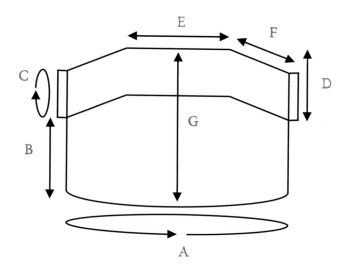

Abbreviations

BO	bind off
BOR	beginning of round
CC	contrasting color
CO	cast on
dec	decrease
DS	double stitch
k	knit
LH	left-hand
MC	main color
p	purl
pm	place marker
rep	repeat
RH	right-hand
RS	right side
sl	slip
sl1p	slip one purlwise
ssk	slip, slip, knit
st(s)	stitch(es)
WS	wrong side
wyif	with yarn in front
yo	yarn over

Pattern

Check out the "Getting the Right Fit" section on page 160 for tips on modifying your sleeve circumference, shoulder seam length or the neckline opening.

Body

Using SMALLER needles and MC, CO 192 (216, 240, 264, **288, 312, 336, 360,** 384, 408, 432) sts.

Note: I recommend working the first two rows of your sweater flat. This will help you to prevent accidentally twisting your CO sts when you join in the round. If you prefer to join in the round right away, skip Rows 1 and 2.

Row 1 (RS): (K1, p1) rep to end.

Row 2 (WS): (K1, p1) rep to end.

Place a BOR marker and join to work in the round.

Ribbing Round: (K1, p1) rep to end.

Rep Ribbing Round until your work measures approximately 1 inch (2.5 cm) from the CO edge.

Change to LARGER needles. Knit every round until your work measures 12 (11.5, 11.25, 10.75, **10.5, 9.75, 9, 8.75,** 8, 7.5, 7) inches [30 (29, 28.5, 27, **26.5, 24.5, 22.5, 22,** 20, 19, 17.5) cm] from the CO edge.

Note: If you would like to add length to your tee, this is the best place to do so.

Division Round: K96 (108, 120, 132, **144, 156, 168, 180,** 192, 204, 216), place the next 96 (108, 120, 132, **144, 156, 168, 180,** 192, 204, 216) sts on a piece of scrap yarn.

You should now have 96 (108, 120, 132, **144, 156, 168, 180,** 192, 204, 216) sts on your needles. These are your Back Yoke sts. You should have 96 (108, 120, 132, **144, 156, 168, 180,** 192, 204, 216) sts on a piece of scrap yarn. These are your Front Yoke sts.

Back Yoke

You will now begin short row shaping. You will no longer be knitting in the round.

Next Row (WS): P to last 3 sts, turn work.

Row 1 (RS): DS, k to last 3 sts, turn work.

With the RS facing you, your live yarn will be at the LH side of the Back Yoke. You will now begin working at the RH edge of your sts.

With the RS facing you, using LARGER needles and CC and the Cable cast on method, CO 33 (35, 36, 39, **41, 45, 48, 51,** 54, 57, 60) sts to the LH needle (at the end of the Back Yoke sts).

> **Note:** The Cable cast on in this pattern is used to attach the CC sts to the MC sts. If you are new to using the Cable cast on in this way, see page 177 for more info.

You should now have 129 (143, 156, 171, **185, 201, 216, 231,** 246, 261, 276) sts on your needles. This will be 96 (108, 120, 132, **144, 156, 168, 180,** 192, 204, 216) MC sts and 33 (35, 36, 39, **41, 45, 48, 51,** 54, 57, 60) CC sts.

Row 1 (RS): K32 (34, 35, 38, **40, 44, 47, 50,** 53, 56, 59), ssk (1 st from CC with 1 st from MC), turn work. [1 st dec]

Row 2 (WS): Sl1p wyif, p to end.

Rep Rows 1 and 2 an additional 24 (30, 36, 42, **46, 52, 57, 63,** 68, 74, 80) times.

Rep Row 1 once more. You have reached the first stitch marker. Remove this stitch marker.

You should now have 103 (111, 118, 127, **137, 147, 157, 166,** 176, 185, 194) sts on your needles. This will be 70 (76, 82, 88, **96, 102, 109, 115,** 122, 128, 134) MC sts and 33 (35, 36, 39, **41, 45, 48, 51,** 54, 57, 60) CC sts.

Set-Up Row (WS): Sl1p wyif, p to last 3 sts, k3.

Row 3 (RS): Sl1p wyif, yo, k2, yo, ssk, k27 (29, 30, 33, **35, 39, 42, 45,** 48, 51, 54), ssk (1 st from CC with 1 st from MC), turn work.

Row 4 (WS): Sl1p wyif, p to last 4 sts, k2, k2tog. [1 st dec]

Rep Rows 3 and 4 an additional 43 (43, 43, 43, **47, 47, 49, 49,** 51, 51, 51) times. You have reached the second st marker. Remove this st marker.

Row 2 (WS): DS, p to last 4 sts before last DS, turn work.

Row 3 (RS): DS, k to last 4 sts before last DS, turn work.

Rep Rows 2 and 3 an additional 4 (5, 5, 6, **6, 7, 8, 9,** 10, 11, 12) times.

Next Row (WS): DS, p to end, resolving all DS sts as you come to them.

Next Row (RS): K26 (32, 38, 44, **48, 54, 59, 65,** 70, 76, 82), pm, k44 (44, 44, 44, **48, 48, 50, 50,** 52, 52, 52), pm, k26 (32, 38, 44, **48, 54, 59, 65,** 70, 76, 82), resolving all DS sts as you come to them.

Break MC, leaving a 6-inch (15-cm) tail.

Back Yoke Border

> **Note:** If your self-striping yardage is limited, or if you do not want to match up stripes using the Mattress Stitch seaming method (see page 183), consider knitting the Back Yoke Border section in your main color.

You should now have 59 (67, 74, 83, **89, 99, 107, 116,** 124, 133, 142) sts on your needles. This will be 26 (32, 38, 44, **48, 54, 59, 65,** 70, 76, 82) MC sts and 33 (35, 36, 39, **41, 45, 48, 51,** 54, 57, 60) CC sts.

Row 5 (RS): K32 (34, 35, 38, **40, 44, 47, 50,** 53, 56, 59), ssk (1 st from CC with 1 st from MC), turn work. [1 st dec]

Row 6 (WS): Sl1p wyif, p to end.

Rep Rows 5 and 6 until one Body st remains on your needles. Rep Row 5 once more.

BO all sts purlwise on a WS row.

> Note: When you BO the CC sts, I recommend slipping the first st rather than purling it. This will create a consistent transition on the RS of your work.

Front Yoke & Front Yoke Border

Using LARGER needles, place sts held for the Front Yoke on your needles. Join MC. You should have 96 (108, 120, 132, **144, 156, 168, 180,** 192, 204, 216) sts on your needles. Beginning on a RS row, join your yarn.

Knit one row.

Work the Front Yoke & Front Yoke Border section according to the instructions for the Back Yoke and Back Yoke Border sections. The Front Yoke will be identical to the Back Yoke, and the Front Yoke Border will be identical to the Back Yoke Border.

> Note: When starting your Front Yoke Border, I recommend starting the striping sequence with the same color stripe that you ended the Back Yoke Border with. Check to make sure that you are working the stripes in the reverse sequence, so that the stripes line up at the top of the shoulders.

Shoulder Seams

> Note: I highly recommend blocking your sweater before seaming the shoulders. Your knitting will relax during wet blocking. This will help you measure the neckline opening more accurately and match up the stripes on the Back and Front Yoke Borders. This will also help you achieve an appropriate tension in the shoulder seams.

You will use the Mattress Stitch seaming method (see page 183) to join the Front Yoke Border to the Back Yoke Border. Lay out the borders with the RS facing you. Measure along the side of each border from the sleeve edge up. Place a removable marker 6.5 (8, 9.5, 11, **12, 13.5, 14.75, 16.25,** 17.5, 19, 20.5) inches [16.5 (20, 24, 27.5, **30, 34, 37, 40.5,** 44, 47.5, 51.5) cm] from the sleeve edge on both the Front Yoke Border and the Back Yoke Border. Use the Mattress Stitch to seam the borders together from the sleeve edge to the removable marker.

> Note: The shoulder seam measurements are based on a row gauge of eight rows / 1 inch (2.5 cm). If your row gauge does not match the gauge listed in the pattern, you will need to adjust the length of the shoulder seam in order to create a flat neckline of 11 (11, 11, 11, **12, 12, 12.5, 12.5,** 13, 13, 13) inches [27.5 (27.5, 27.5, 27.5, **30, 30, 31.5, 31.5,** 32.5, 32.5, 32.5) cm]. See the "Getting the Right Fit" section on page 160.

Sleeve Cuffs

Use SMALLER needles and MC. Beginning at the middle of the underarm, pick up and knit 68 (72, 74, 80, **84, 92, 98, 104,** 110, 116, 122) sts evenly around the armhole opening. Place a BOR marker.

Ribbing Round: (K1, p1) rep to end.

Rep Ribbing Round until the Sleeve Cuff measures 1 inch (2.5 cm). BO all sts in pattern. Break yarn, leaving a 6-inch (15-cm) tail.

Finishing

Before you weave in your ends, try on your sweater. If you need to make modifications to the neckline length, see the "Getting the Right Fit" section. Once you are happy with the fit of your sweater, weave in all ends. For the best results, be sure to wet block your finished sweater. Soak the sweater in cold water, squeezing to remove air bubbles. Squeeze out the water, but do not wring. Roll the sweater in a dry towel, burrito-style, and press on it to remove excess water. Lay the sweater flat to dry, using a measuring tape to be sure it is laid out with the correct dimensions.

Getting the Right Fit

Modifying Your Sleeve Circumference

In order to modify your sleeve circumference, you will need to add or subtract sts from the Back and Front Yoke Borders. You will need to CO the same number of sts for both the Back and Front Yoke Borders. Every 6 sts that you add/subtract from the border sections (3 sts for the Front Border and 3 sts for the Back Border) will adjust the circumference of the sleeve by 1 inch (2.5 cm). I recommend choosing your preferred sleeve circumference from one of the other sizes. For example, if you would like to work a sleeve circumference of 13 inches (32.5 cm), then you would follow the directions for the Back Yoke Border, Front Yoke Border and Sleeve Cuff sections according to size L. You will work the Shoulder Seam section according to your own size.

Modifying Your Shoulder Seam Length

In order to modify your shoulder seam length, find the center of your Front Yoke Border. Measure out from the center point 5.5 (5.5, 5.5, 5.5, **6, 6, 6.25, 6.25,** 6.5, 6.5, 6.5) inches [13.75 (13.75, 13.75, 13.75, **15, 15, 15.5, 15.5,** 16.5, 16.5, 16.5) cm] in both directions. Place a removable st marker to the left and right of the center point, according to your neckline measurement. Repeat for the Back Yoke Border. Use the Mattress Stitch (see page 183) to seam the borders together from the sleeve edge to the removable marker.

Modifying Your Neckline

This pattern is designed with a wide boatneck to create an airy, summery top. However, if you would prefer a smaller neckline opening, you can adjust the length of the shoulder seams in order to reduce the size of the neckline. To begin, find the center of your Front Yoke Border. Measure out from the center point one half of your desired neckline opening in both directions. Place a removable stitch marker to the left and right of the center point, according to your neckline measurement. Repeat for the Back Yoke Border. You will now seam your work from the sleeve edge to the removable marker.

> Note: Because the neck opening has a slipped st edge, you may find it difficult to work the Mattress Stitch when you reach the slipped sts. If you find this to be the case, I recommend using the whip stitch or back stitch on the WS of your work to seam the slipped sts together.

Modifying the Length of Your Sweater

This tee was designed to be slightly cropped. If you would prefer to add length to your tee, I recommend adding additional knit rounds in the Body section before dividing the stitches to work the Back Yoke. Before you add length to your tee, measure from your suprasternal notch (the dip between your collar bones and approximately where your neckline will land when you wear your tee) down to your waist. Find your ideal stopping point for your tee on your measuring tape. Compare this length to the total length for your size in the Finished Measurements. Adjust the Body of your tee to your desired measurements.

Drop a Rainbow Pullover
Skill Level: Intermediate

I sometimes get addicted to a sweater. I will wear one sweater over and over, day after day, until my kids start to ask what happened to my other clothes. No matter what else is in my closet, I have a hard time putting on anything else. The Drop a Rainbow Pullover is an addictive sweater. Like the Sock Arms Cardigan, this pullover uses self-striping yarn in the sleeves, but this time with a more casual drop shoulder construction. In the Drop a Rainbow Pullover, all the short row shaping is worked in the body of this sweater, making the sleeves happily low maintenance. A flattering spiral is worked around each sleeve to add a little twist to your self-striping yarn and hide the decreases. To get the right fit for you, Refer to the "How to Modifiy Your Sleeve Circumference" section on page 169.

Construction

This pullover is knit flat to create a front and back hem. After completing both hems, the hems are joined and the body is worked in the round. The front and back yokes are divided and worked separately and flat. The shoulders are shaped using the German Short Rows method (see page 184) and then joined using a three-needle bind off (see page 180). The sleeves are then picked up around the armhole and worked in the round. Finally, the collar stitches are picked up and worked in the round.

Maximum Stitches Used for a Self-Striping Round:
58 (60, 64, 72, **80, 86, 92,** 98, 100, 104)

Sizes

XS (S, M, L, **XL, 2XL, 3XL,** 4XL, 5XL, 6XL)

See the Finished Measurements on page 163 to choose your size.

NOTE: Throughout this pattern you will find that **sizes XL, 2XL and 3XL** appear in bold type. Use this indicator to help you easily find your size as you navigate the pattern.

Yarn

- DK weight yarn, Louise Robert Design DK Pure
- (90% superwash merino and 10% silk, 260 yards / 4 ounces [237 m / 115 g]), MC
- DK weight yarn, Biscotte Yarns DK Pure
- (90% superwash merino and 10% silk, 260 yards / 4 ounces [237 m / 115 g]), CC
- 3 (3, 3, 3, **4, 4, 4,** 4, 4, 5) skeins of MC and 2 (2, 2, 2, **2, 2, 3,** 3, 3, 3) skeins of CC
- Sample shown in "Ann Boleyn" (MC, deep purple) and "Carousel" (CC, self-striping)
- **Main Color:** 550 (590, 650, 710, **790, 860, 900,** 960, 1015, 1075) yards / [503 (540, 595, 650, **723, 787, 823,** 878, 928, 983) m]
- **Contrasting Color:** 310 (335, 360, 400, **465, 490, 520,** 570, 595, 620) yards / [284 (306, 329, 366, **425, 448, 475,** 521, 544, 567) m]

Yarn Notes

This pattern was knit using a DK weight merino and silk blend. The small amount of silk in this yarn gives it a subtle sheen. If you prefer a denser fabric, consider using a worsted weight yarn.

Needles

US 6 (4 mm) 32-inch (80-cm) circulars (length as appropriate for your size), or as required to meet gauge

US 5 (5.75 mm) 16-inch (40-cm) circulars

DPNs or needles for small circumference in both size needles

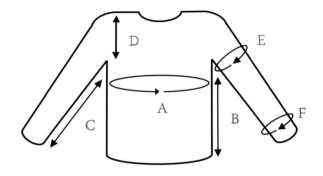

Gauge

20 stitches and 28 rounds = 4 inches (10 cm) in stockinette stitch on LARGER needles after blocking

Notions

- 2 stitch markers
- Scissors
- Scrap yarn
- Tapestry needle
- Tape measure

Finished Measurements

Sample shown is a size M with 6 inches (15 cm) of positive ease at the bust. I recommend 6 to 8 inches (15 to 20 cm) of ease at the bust for this pullover.

A. **Bust:** 32.5 (36.5, 38, 42, **46, 50, 56.5,** 60.5, 64.5, 68.5) inches / [81.5 (91, 95, 105, **115, 125, 141,** 151, 161, 171) cm]

B. **Length of Body (Hem to Underarm):** 15 inches (37.5 cm)

C. **Sleeve Length:** 17.5 inches (44 cm)

D. **Yoke Depth:** 5.75 (6, 6.5, 7.5, **8, 8.75, 9.25,** 9.75, 10, 10.5) inches / [14.5 (15, 16, 19, **20, 22, 23,** 24.5, 25, 26.5) cm]

E. **Sleeve Circumference:** 11.5 (12, 13, 14.5, **16, 17.25, 18.5,** 19.5, 20, 21) inches / [29 (30, 32.5, 36.5, **40, 43, 46,** 49, 50, 52.5) cm]

F. **Wrist Circumference:** 10 (10, 10.75, 10.75, **11.5, 12.5, 13.25,** 14, 14, 10) inches / [25 (25, 27, 27, **29, 31, 33,** 35, 35, 35) cm]

Abbreviations	
BO	bind off
BOR	beginning of round
CC	contrasting color
CO	cast on
dec	decrease
DS	double stitch
inc	increase
k	knit
k2tog	knit two together
k3tog	knit three together
MC	main color
m1L	make one left
m1R	make one right
p	purl
p2tog	purl two together
rep	repeat
RH	right-hand
RS	right side
sl1p	slip one purlwise
ssk	slip, slip, knit
sssk	slip, slip, slip, knit
st(s)	stitch(es)
WS	wrong side
wyif	with yarn in front
yo	yarn over

Pattern

Back Hem

Using LARGER needles and MC, CO 81 (91, 95, 105, **115, 125, 141,** 151, 161, 171) sts.

Row 1 (RS): Sl1p wyif, yo, k to end. [1 st inc]

Row 2 (WS): Sl1p wyif, yo, k to last 2 sts, k2tog.

Row 3 (RS): Sl1p wyif, yo, k to last 2 sts, k2tog.

Rep Rows 2 and 3 an additional eleven times to create twelve garter ridges. End after completing a RS row. Rep Row 2 once more.

Next Row (RS): Sl1p wyif, k to last 2 sts, k2tog. [1 st dec]

Next Row (WS): Sl1p wyif, k to end.

Place sts on a piece of scrap yarn or spare needles. Break yarn, leaving a 6-inch (15-cm) tail.

Front Hem

Using LARGER needles and MC, CO 81 (91, 95, 105, **115, 125, 141,** 151, 161, 171) sts.

Row 1 (RS): Sl1p wyif, yo, k to end. [1 st inc]

Row 2 (WS): Sl1p wyif, yo, k to last 2 sts, k2tog.

Row 3 (RS): Sl1p wyif, yo, k to last 2 sts, k2tog.

Rep Rows 2 and 3 an additional three times to create four garter ridges, end after completing a RS row. Rep Row 2 once more.

Next Row (RS): Sl1p wyif, k to last 2 sts, k2tog. [1 st dec]

Next Row (WS): Sl1p wyif, k to end.

Do not break yarn.

Body

Set-Up Round: With the RS facing you, k81 (91, 95, 105, **115, 125, 141,** 151, 161, 171) sts across the front hem, join the back hem with the RS facing you and k81 (91, 95, 105, **115, 125, 141,** 151, 161, 171) sts across back hem. Place a BOR marker and join to work in the round. [162 (182, 190, 210, **230, 250, 282,** 302, 322, 342) sts total]

Work in stockinette stitch (k every round) until the body measures 15 inches (37.5 cm) from the CO edge of the front hem.

Dividing for the Yoke

You will now divide the body stitches into the front and back yokes.

Yoke Division Round: K81 (91, 95, 105, **115, 125, 141,** 151, 161, 171) sts, place the next k81 (91, 95, 105, **115, 125, 141,** 151, 161, 171) sts onto a piece of scrap yarn.

You will now turn your work in order to work a WS row. You will no longer be working in the round. You will now begin working flat.

You should now have 81 (91, 95, 105, **115, 125, 141,** 151, 161, 171) sts on your needles. These are your Front Yoke sts. You should have 81 (91, 95, 105, **115, 125, 141,** 151, 161, 171) sts on a piece of scrap yarn. These are your Back Yoke sts.

Front Yoke

Work in stockinette stitch (k the RS rows, p the WS rows) until the Front Yoke measures 4 (4.25, 4.5, 5, **5.5, 5.5, 6,** 6.5, 6.75, 7) inches [10 (10.5, 11.5, 12.5, **14, 14, 15,** 16.5, 17, 17.5) cm] from the underarm division. End after completing a WS row.

Front of the Neck Shaping

Row 1 (Neck Shaping Set-Up Row) (RS): K35 (39, 41, 45, **50, 55, 62,** 67, 71, 76), BO 11 (13, 13, 15, **15, 15, 17,** 17, 19, 19), k to end.

You have two sets of 35 (39, 41, 45, **50, 55, 62,** 67, 71, 76) sts on your needles. Place the first set of 35 (39, 41, 45, **50, 55, 62,** 67, 71, 76) sts on a piece of scrap yarn for the Front Left Shoulder.

Front Right Shoulder

Row 2 (WS): P to last 3 sts, ssp, p1. [1 st dec]

Row 3 (RS): K1, ssk, k to end. [1 st dec]

Rep Rows 2 and 3 until you have 31 (35, 35, 37, **40, 45, 52,** 57, 61, 64) sts.

Row 4 (WS): P all.

Row 5 (RS): K1, ssk, k to end. [1 st dec]

Rep Rows 4 and 5 until you have 27 (31, 31, 33, **36, 39, 46,** 51, 55, 58) sts.

You will now begin short row shaping the shoulder:

Row 6 (WS): P all.

Row 7 (RS): K to last 5 sts, turn work.

Rows 8 (WS): DS, p to end.

Row 9 (RS): K to 5 sts before last DS, turn work.

Work Rows 8 and 9 an additional 1 (1, 1, 1, **2, 2, 2,** 2, 3, 3) time(s). End after completing a RS row.

Next Row (WS): DS, p to end.

Next Row (RS): K, resolving all DS sts as you come to them.

Break yarn, leaving a 30-inch (76-cm) tail. Place sts on a piece of scrap yarn for three-needle bind off later.

Front Left Shoulder

Place the held sts on your LARGER needles. Beginning on a WS row, join your MC.

> Note: Row 1 was worked at the beginning of the Front of the Neck Shaping section.

Row 2 (WS): P1, p2tog, p to end. [1 st dec]

Row 3 (RS): K to last 3 sts, k2tog, k. [1 st dec]

Rep Rows 2 and 3 until you have 31 (35, 35, 37, **40, 45, 52,** 57, 61, 64) sts.

Row 4 (WS): P all.

Row 5 (RS): K to last 3 sts, k2tog, k1. [1 st dec]

Rep Rows 4 and 5 until you have 27 (31, 31, 33, **36, 39, 46,** 51, 55, 58) sts.

You will now begin short row shaping the shoulder:

Row 6 (WS): P to last 5 sts, turn work.

Row 7 (RS): DS, k to end.

Rows 8 (WS): P to 5 sts before last DS, turn work.

Row 9 (RS): DS, k to end.

Work Rows 8 and 9 an additional 1 (1, 1, 1, **2, 2, 2,** 2, 3, 3) time(s). End after completing a RS row.

Next Row (WS): P, resolving all DS sts as you come to them.

Next Row (RS): K all.

Break yarn, leaving a 30-inch (76-cm) tail. Place sts on a piece of scrap yarn for three-needle bind off later.

Back Yoke

Place the 81 (91, 95, 105, **115, 125, 141,** 151, 161, 171) sts held for the Back Yoke on your LARGER needles. Beginning on a WS row, work in stockinette stitch (k the RS rows, p the WS rows) until the Back Yoke measures 5.75 (6, 6.5, 7.25, **8, 8.75, 9.25,** 9.75, 10, 10.5) inches / [14.5 (15, 16.5, 18, **20, 22, 23,** 24.5, 25, 26.5) cm] from the underarm division. End after completing a WS row.

Back Shoulders

Row 1 (Neck Shaping Set-Up Row) (RS): K36 (40, 40, 42, **48, 51, 58,** 63, 70, 73), BO 9 (11, 15, 21, **19, 23, 25,** 25, 21, 25), k to end.

You have two sets of 36 (40, 40, 42, **48, 51, 58,** 63, 70, 73) sts on your needles. Place the first set of 36 (40, 40, 42, **48, 51, 58,** 63, 70, 73) sts on a piece of scrap yarn for Back Right Shoulder.

Back Left Shoulder

Row 2 (WS): P all.

Row 3 (RS): BO 3 knitwise, k to last 5 sts, turn work. [3 sts dec]

Row 4 (WS): DS, p to end.

Row 5 (RS): BO 3 knitwise, k to 5 sts before last DS, turn work. [3 sts dec]

Rep Rows 4 and 5 until you have 27 (31, 31, 33, **36, 39, 46,** 51, 55, 58) sts.

Next Row (WS): DS, p to end.

Next Row (RS): K, picking up wrapped sts as you come to them.

Turn your work so that the RS are facing in and WS are facing out. Align the Front Left Shoulder to the Back Left Shoulder. With the front of the sweater facing you, work three-needle bind off. Break yarn, leaving a 6-inch (15-cm) tail.

Back Right Shoulder

Place the held sts on your LARGER needles. Beginning on a RS row, join your MC.

Row 1 (RS): K all.

Row 2 (WS): BO 3 purlwise, p to last 5 sts, turn work. [3 sts dec]

Row 3 (RS): DS, k to end.

Row 4 (WS): BO 3 purlwise, p to 5 sts before last DS, turn work. [3 sts dec]

Rep Rows 3 and 4 until you have 27 (31, 31, 33, **36, 39, 46,** 51, 55, 58) sts.

Next Row (RS): DS, k to end.

Next Row (WS): P, resolving all DS sts as you come to them.

Do not break yarn. Turn your work so that the RS are facing in and WS are facing out. Align the Front Right Shoulder to the Back Right Shoulder. With the front of the sweater facing you, work three-needle bind off. Break yarn, leaving a 6-inch (15-cm) tail.

Right Sleeve

> Note: The Right Sleeve refers to the RH side of the sweater as worn. That is, when your sweater is complete, this sleeve will be worn on your right arm.

Use CC and LARGER needles for small circumference knitting. Beginning at the middle of the underarm, pick up and knit 29 (30, 32, 36, **40, 43, 46,** 49, 50, 52) sts between the center of the underarm and the top of the shoulder. Place a marker. Pick up and knit 29 (30, 32, 36, **40, 43, 46,** 49, 50, 52) sts between the top of the shoulder and the center of the underarm. You will be picking up approximately 3 of 4 sts.

> Note: You may need to make minor adjustments to the ratio in order to pick up the appropriate number of sts for your sleeve. Place a BOR marker and join to work in the round.

You should now have 58 (60, 64, 72, **80, 86, 92,** 98, 100, 104) sts on your needles.

> Note: Throughout this section, the BOR marker will remain next to the first decrease stitch. However, the marker will not stay at the underarm, because of the combination of decreases and increases. In order to differentiate the BOR marker from the second marker, I suggest using two different colored markers while working the Sleeve and making a note of which marker is the BOR marker.

Rounds 1-10 (10. 10. 10. **8. 8. 8.** 6. 6. 6): (Ssk, k to 1 st before m, m1R, k1, sm) 2 times.

Round 11 (11. 11. 11. **9. 9. 9.** 7. 7. 7): (Sssk, k to 1 st before m, m1R, k1, sm) 2 times. [2 sts dec]

Rep Rounds 1-11 (11, 11, 11, **9, 9, 9,** 7, 7, 7) until you have 50 (50, 54, 54, **58, 62, 66,** 70, 70, 70) sts on your needles.

Rep Round 1 until your sleeve measures 16.5 inches (41.5 cm) or 1 inch (2.5 cm) less than your desired length.

Break CC, leaving a 6-inch (15-cm) tail. Join MC.

Change to SMALLER needles.

Cuff Round 1: K to m, sm, k to end.

Cuff Round 2: (K1, p to 1 st before m, k1, sm) twice.

Rep Cuff Rounds 1 and 2 until cuff measures 1 inch (2.5 cm), or desired length.

BO all sts knitwise and break yarn, leaving a 6-inch (15-cm) tail.

Round 1-10 (10, 10, 10, **8, 8, 8,** 6, 6, 6): (K1, m1L, k to 2 sts before m, k2tog, sm) 2 times.

Round 11 (11, 11, 11, **9, 9, 9,** 7, 7, 7): (K1, m1L, k to 3 sts before m, k3tog, sm) 2 times. [2 sts dec]

Rep Rounds 1–11 (11, 11, 11, **9, 9, 9,** 7, 7, 7) until you have 50 (50, 54, 54, **58, 62, 66,** 70, 70, 70) sts on your needles.

Rep Round 1 until your sleeve measures 16.5 inches (41.5 cm) or 1 inch (2.5 cm) less than your desired length.

Break CC, leaving a 6-inch (15-cm) tail. Join MC.

Change to SMALLER needles.

Cuff Round 1: K to m, sm, k to end.

Cuff Round 2: (K1, p to 1 st before m, k1, sm) twice.

Rep Cuff Rounds 1 and 2 until cuff measures 1 inch (2.5 cm), or desired length.

BO all sts knitwise and break yarn, leaving a 6-inch (15-cm) tail.

Left Sleeve

Use CC and LARGER needles for small circumference knitting. Beginning at the middle of the underarm, pick up and knit 29 (30, 32, 36, **40, 43, 46,** 49, 50, 52) sts between the center of the underarm and the top of the shoulder. Place a marker. Pick up and knit 29 (30, 32, 36, **40, 43, 46,** 49, 50, 52) sts between the top of the shoulder and the center of the underarm. You will be picking up approximately 3 of 4 sts.

You should now have 58 (60, 64, 72, **80, 86, 92,** 98, 100, 104) sts on your needles.

Collar

Begin at the left back neck. Using MC and SMALLER needles, pick up and knit 3 sts for every four rows down the slope of the neck, all sts across the front neck, 3 sts for every four rows up the slope of the neck and all sts across the back of the neck. End with an even number of sts. Place a BOR marker and join to work in the round.

Work 1x1 ribbing (k1, p1) until collar measures 1 inch (2.5 cm), or desired length. BO all sts in pattern, leaving a 6-inch (15-cm) tail.

Finishing

Weave in all ends. For the best results, be sure to wet block your finished sweater. Soak the sweater in cold water, squeezing to remove air bubbles. Squeeze out the water, but do not wring. Roll the sweater in a dry towel, burrito-style, and press on it to remove excess water. Lay the sweater flat to dry, using a measuring tape to be sure it is laid out with the correct dimensions.

How to Modify Your Sleeve Circumference:

You may find that you would like to add to the circumference of the sleeves of your sweater. The best way to do this is to add length to the yoke of the sweater, so that you have more space to pick up sts when you reach the sleeves. You can use the following steps to modify your sleeves. Please remember that changes to the finished dimensions will result in changes to your final yardage.

> **Note:** If you would like to reduce the size of your sleeves, you will follow the same steps outlined below. However, in Step 3, you will get a negative result. Rather than adding additional length to the Front Yoke and Back Yoke, simply subtract this amount from the total stockinette length for your size.

Step 1: First, find the bust size and the sleeve circumference you want to knit in the Finished Dimensions measurements on page 163.

For example, let's say that I want a sweater with a 56.5-inch (141-cm) bust (size 3XL) and 19.5-inch (49-cm) sleeve circumference (size 4XL).

Step 2: Work the Back Hem, Front Hem, Body and Dividing for the Yoke sections according to your target bust measurement.

In this example, I would work these four sections according to the instructions for size 3XL.

Step 3: Find the difference between the sleeves for your target bust size and the sleeves for your target sleeve size and divide the length in half. Then, add this length to the total stockinette worked at the beginning of the Front Yoke section.

In my example sweater, the sleeve circumference for the sweater in my bust size (3XL) is 18.5 inches (46 cm). The sleeve circumference for my target sleeves (4XL) is 19.5 inches (49 cm). I then subtract 18.5 inches (46 cm) from 19.5 inches (49 cm) for a total of 1 inch (2.5 cm). I divide this amount in half for a total of 0.5 inches (1.25 cm). This is my magic number. Finally, I would add 0.5 inches (1.25 cm) of stockinette to the stockinette section at the beginning of the Front Yoke.

Step 4: Work the remaining Front Yoke, Front Right Shoulder and Front Left Shoulder sections according to your bust measurement.

For this example, I would work these sections according to size 3XL.

Step 5: Add the same amount of stockinette in the Back Yoke section that you added to the Front Yoke. This will be the same magical number you found in Step 3.

I will work an additional 0.5 inches (1.25 cm) of stockinette at the beginning of the Back Yoke in my example sweater.

Step 6: Work the remaining Back Yoke, Back Left Shoulder and Back Right Shoulder sections according to your bust measurement.

For this example, I would work these sections according to size 3XL.

Step 7: Work the Right Sleeve and Left Sleeve sections according to your target sleeve measurement.

In this example, I would work 4XL sleeves.

Backlit Tee

Skill Level: Intermediate

Stranded colorwork and self-striping yarn is a magical combination. When you pair an already beautiful self-striping yarn with a solid, the self-striping yarn comes to life in a way that it never would on its own. It seems to glow, as if magically lit from beneath. The Backlit Tee was designed to amplify this enchanting glow with all-over colorwork. Let the self-striping yarn do all the work while you zip through a relaxing project with minimal ends to weave in. Knit seamlessly in the round from the top down, this tee was designed to wow.

Construction

This tee is worked seamlessly from the top down using stranded colorwork. After completing the yoke, the sleeves are placed on hold and the body is completed. Finally, the sleeve stitches are placed back on the needles and worked in the round.

Maximum Stitches Used for a Self-Striping Round: 320 (350, 390, 430, **450, 490, 530,** 570, 590, 640)

Sizes

XS (S, M, L, **XL, 2XL, 3XL,** 4XL, 5XL, 6XL)

See the Finished Measurements on page 172 to choose your size.

NOTE: Throughout this pattern you will find that **sizes XL, 2XL and 3XL** appear in bold type. Use this indicator to help you easily find your size as you navigate the pattern.

Yarn

- Fingering weight yarn, Fab Funky Fibres
- (75% superwash merino and 25% nylon, 370 yards / 80g)
- Sample shown in "Naked" (MC, white) and "Walking on Rainbows" (CC, self-striping)
- 2 (2, 2, 2, **3, 3, 3,** 3, 3, 3) skeins of MC and 1 (1, 1, 1, **2, 2, 2,** 2, 2, 3) skeins of CC
- **Main Color:** 575 (625, 670, 710, **760, 860, 900,** 940, 990, 1050) yards / [526 (572, 613, 650, **695, 732, 823,** 860, 905, 960) m]
- **Contrasting Color:** 275 (300, 325, 375, **410, 440, 475,** 510, 550, 600) yards / [252 (275, 297, 343, **375, 403, 435,** 466, 503, 549) m]

Yarn Notes

This pattern was knit using a self-striping yarn that has a gradient effect, in which one color changes gradually into another. This gradation allows for subtle color changes on the longer rows.

Needles

US 6 (4 mm) 24- or 32-inch (60- or 80-cm) circular (as appropriate for your size), or as required to meet gauge

US 5 (3.75 mm) 24- or 32-inch (60- or 80-cm) circular (as appropriate for your size)

DPNs or needles for small circumference in the same sizes

Gauge

24 stitches and 28 rounds = 4 inches (10 cm) in stockinette stitch AND in stockinette stitch in colorwork motif on LARGER needles

Notions

- 1 stitch marker
- Scissors
- Tapestry needle
- Scrap yarn
- Tape measure

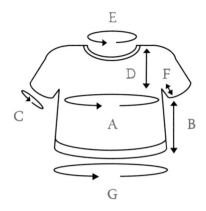

Abbreviations	
BO	bind off
BOR	beginning of round
CC	contrasting color
CO	cast on
dec	decrease
inc	increase
k	knit
m	marker
m1L	make one left
MC	main color
p	purl
rep	repeat
RS	right side
sm	slip marker
st(s)	stitch(es)
WS	wrong side
w&t	wrap and turn

Finished Measurements

Sample shown is a size M with 7 inches (17.5 cm) of positive ease at the bust. I recommend 4 to 10 inches (10 to 25 cm) of ease at the bust for this tee. Please note that the yoke depth is measured from the back of the neck.

A. **Bust:** 35.25 (39.25, 43.25, 47.25, **51.25, 55.25, 59.25,** 63.25, 67.25, 71.25) inches / [88 (98, 108, 118, **128, 138, 148,** 158, 168, 178) cm]

B. **Length of Body (Hem to Underarm):** 11 inches (27.5 cm)

C. **Sleeve Circumference:** 10.75 (11.25, 12.5, 14, **15.25, 16.5, 18,** 19.25, 20.5, 22.75) inches / [26.5 (28, 31.5, 35, **38, 41.5, 45,** 48, 51.5, 56.5) cm]

D. **Yoke Depth:** 8.75 (8.75, 8.75, 9.25, **9.25, 9.25, 9.75,** 9.75, 10.25, 10.25) inches / [22 (22, 22, 23, **23, 23, 24.5,** 24.5, 25.5, 25.5) cm]

E. **Neckline Circumference:** 16.75 (18, 19.25, 20, **20.75, 22, 22,** 23.25, 23.25, 23.25) inches / [41.5 (45, 48.5, 50, **51.5, 55, 55,** 58.5, 58.5, 58.5) cm]

F. **Sleeve Length:** 4.5 inch (9.5 cm)

G. **Hem Circumference:** 36 (40, 44, 48, **52, 56, 60,** 64, 68, 72) inches / [90 (100, 110, 120, **130, 140, 150,** 160, 170, 180) cm]

Pattern

Yoke

Using SMALLER needles and MC, CO 100 (108, 116, 120, **124, 132, 132,** 140, 140, 140) sts. Place a BOR marker and join to work in the round.

> Note: The BOR marker is placed at the center back of your work.

Work 2x2 ribbing (k2, p2) for four rounds. Change to LARGER needles.

Neckline Increase Round 1:

Sizes XS, S, M, L and XL: (K4, m1L) rep to end. [25 (27, 29, 30, **31, -, -,** -, -, -) sts inc; 125 (135, 145, 150, **155, -, -,** -, -, -) sts total]

Size 2XL: (K3, m1L) rep to end. [44 sts inc; 176 sts total]

Size 3XL, 4XL, 5XL and 6XL: (K2, m1L) rep to end. [- (-, -, -, **-, -, 66,** 70, 70, 70) sts inc; - (-, -, -, **-, -, 198,** 210, 210, 210) sts total]

Knit one round.

Neckline Short Row Shaping:

You will now work short rows in order to raise the back of the neckline for a better fitting sweater.

Row 1 (RS): Beginning at the BOR m, k38 (42, 46, 52, **54, 58, 64,** 68, 70, 76), w&t.

Row 2 (WS): P to BOR m, sm, p38 (42, 46, 52, **54, 58, 64,** 68, 70, 76), w&t.

Row 3 (RS): K to 5 sts before last wrapped st, w&t.

Row 4 (WS): P to 5 sts before last wrapped st, w&t.

Rep Rows 3 and 4 an additional 2 (2, 2, 2, **2, 3, 3,** 3, 3, 3) times.

> Note: See page 184 for information on how to work Wrap & Turn Short Rows.

Row 5 (RS): K to BOR m.

You will now resume working in the round.

Next Round: K all, working wraps together with wrapped sts as you come to them.

Neckline Increase Round 2:

Size XS: (K41, m1L) 3 times, k2. [3 sts inc; 128 sts total]

Size S: (K27, m1L) 5 times. [5 sts inc; 140 sts total]

Size M: (K13, m1L) 11 times, k2. [11 sts inc; 156 sts total]

Size L: (M1L, k7) 21 times, m1L, k3. [22 sts inc; 172 sts total]

Size XL: (K6, m1L) 25 times, k5. [25 sts inc; 180 sts total]

Size 2XL: (M1L, k9) 19 times, m1L, k5. [20 sts inc; 196 sts total]

Size 3XL: (K14, m1L) 14 times, k2. [14 sts inc; 212 sts total]

Size 4XL: (M1L, k12) 17 times, m1L, k6. [18 sts inc; 228 sts total]

Size 5XL: (K8, m1L) 26 times, k2. [26 sts inc; 236 sts total]

Size 6XL: (M1L, k5) 26 times, (m1L, k4) rep 20 times. [46 sts inc; 256 sts total]

Knit one round.

Colorwork

Join CC and work the Yoke Chart on page 176 according to your size.

> Note: Many knitters have a tighter gauge when working in stranded colorwork versus standard stockinette stitch. You may find it necessary to go up a needle size while working the colorwork charts. Verify your colorwork gauge before proceeding. Remember to carry CC loosely on the WS of your work.

After completing the Yoke Chart, you will have 320 (350, 390, 430, **450, 490, 530,** 570, 590, 640) sts on your needles.

Yoke Division

Division Round: Using MC, k50 (56, 62, 68, **72, 78, 84,** 90, 93, 99), CO 5 (5, 5, 5, **10, 10, 10,** 10, 15, 15), sl59 (62, 70, 78, **81, 89, 97,** 105, 108, 121) sts onto a piece of scrap yarn, k101 (113, 125, 137, **144, 156, 168,** 180, 187, 199), CO 5 (5, 5, 5, **10, 10, 10,** 10, 15, 15), sl59 (62, 70, 78, **81, 89, 97,** 105, 108, 121) sts onto a piece of scrap yarn, k51 (57, 63, 69, **72, 78 84,** 90, 94, 100).

You should now have 212 (236, 260, 284, **308, 332, 356,** 380, 404, 428) sts on your needles. These are your Body sts. You should have 59 (62, 70, 78, **81, 89, 97,** 105, 108, 121) sts on two pieces of scrap yarn. These are your Sleeve sts.

Body

Using MC, knit two rounds.

Using MC and CC, work Rounds 1–8 of Body & Sleeve Chart on page 176 until your tee measures approximately 7.5 inches (19 cm) from the underarm or approximately 3.5 inches (9 cm) less than desired length. End after completing either Row 3 or 7 of the Body & Sleeve Chart.

> Note: If you would like to add length to your sweater, this is a great place to do so. Simply add additional repeats of the Body & Sleeve Chart before moving on to the Hem Chart. Remember, changes in length will result in changes to your final yardage.

Hem Chart Set-Up Round: Using MC, [k53 (59, 65, 71, **77, 83, 89,** 95, 101, 107), m1L] 4 times. [4 sts inc; 216 (240, 264, 288, **312, 336, 360,** 384, 408, 432) sts total]

Work Rounds 1–14 of the Body Hem Chart on page 176. Break CC, leaving a 6-inch (15-cm) tail. Continue to work in MC only.

Knit two rounds. Change to SMALLER needles. Work 2x2 ribbing (k2, p2) until the Body measures approximately 11 inches (27.5 cm) from the underarm or desired length. BO all sts in pattern. Break MC, leaving a 6-inch (15-cm) tail.

Sleeves (both worked identically)

Using MC and LARGER needles for small circumference knitting, beginning at the middle of the underarm, pick up and knit 2 (2, 2, 2, **5, 5, 5,** 5, 7, 7) sts. Knit all live sts from your scrap yarn. Pick up and knit 3 (3, 3, 3, **5, 5, 5,** 5, 8, 8) sts from the underarm. Place marker and join in the round.

You should have 64 (67, 75, 83, **91, 99, 107,** 115, 123, 136) sts on your needles.

Sizes S, M, L, XL, 2XL, 3XL, 4XL and 5XL: M1L, k to end. [1 st inc; - (68, 76, 84, **92, 100, 108,** 116, 124, -) sts total]

Sizes XS and 6XL: K all.

Join CC. Using MC and CC, work Rounds 1–8 of Body & Sleeve Chart on page 176 until your sleeve measures approximately 3 inches (7.5 cm) from the underarm or approximately 1.5 inches (4 cm) less than desired length. End after completing either Row 3 or 7 of the Body & Sleeve Chart.

Work Rounds 1–3 of the Sleeve Hem Chart on page 176. Break CC, leaving a 6-inch (15-cm) tail. Continue to work in MC only.

Knit two rounds.

Change to SMALLER needles for small circumference knitting. Work 2x2 ribbing (k2, p2) for four rounds. BO all sts in pattern. Break yarn, leaving a 6-inch (15-cm) tail.

Finishing

Weave in all ends. For the best results, be sure to wet block your finished sweater. Soak the sweater in cold water, squeezing to remove air bubbles. Squeeze out the water, but do not wring. Roll the sweater in a dry towel, burrito-style, and press on it to remove excess water. Lay the sweater flat to dry, using a measuring tape to be sure it is laid out with the correct dimensions.

Chart Instructions

To work the charts, begin at the bottom right corner and work right to left.

Work Yoke Chart 32 (35, 39, 43, **45, 49, 53,** 57, 59, 64) times total.

Work Body Chart 53 (59, 65, 71, **77, 83, 89,** 95, 101, 107) times total.

Work Body Hem Chart 27 (30, 33, 36, **39, 42, 45,** 48 51, 54) times total.

Work Sleeve Chart 16 (17, 19, 21, **23, 25, 27,** 29, 31, 34) times total.

Work Sleeve Hem Chart 16 (17, 19, 21, **23, 25, 27,** 29, 31, 34) times total.

(Continued)

Yoke Sizes XS, S & M

Yoke Sizes L, XL & 2XL

Yoke Sizes 3XL & 4XL

Yoke Sizes 5XL & 6XL

Key

- knit
- Main Color
- Contrasting Color
- m1L
- no stitch

Tee Body Hem

Tee Body & Sleeve

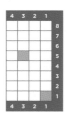

Sleeve Hem

Techniques

In order to get the best results using your self-striping yarn, it is important to use the right techniques. Throughout this book, I have recommended specific cast ons, bind offs, increases, decreases and more. The techniques in these pages aren't flashy or unusual. In fact, these are the same techniques that you would use for knitting projects with (less exciting) non-self-striping yarn. These are the techniques that I have found, through knitting and testing, will give you the best results with your self-striping skeins. Use these step-by-step photos and straightforward instructions to create flawless rainbow knits every time you put yarn on your needles.

Cast Ons & Bind Offs

Backwards Loop Cast On

Step 1: Hold the yarn wrapped over your left thumb.

Step 2: With your right-hand needle, come in front of the thumb and under the yarn.

Step 3: Release the thumb from the loop and pull the yarn snugly to form a stitch on your right-hand needle.

Repeat Steps 1 to 3 until you have cast on the appropriate number of stitches.

Cable Cast On

Step 1: Insert the right-hand needle between the first and second sts on your left-hand needle.

Step 2: Wrap your yarn around the needle as if to knit and pull the new st through.

Step 3: Slip the new stitch on your right-hand needle onto your left-hand needle.

Repeat Steps 1 through 3 until you have cast on the appropriate number of stitches.

Backwards Loop Cast On

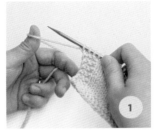

Cable Cast On

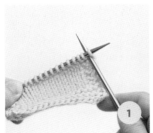

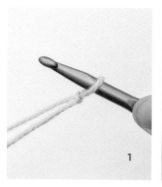

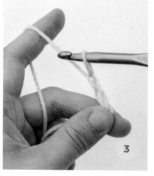

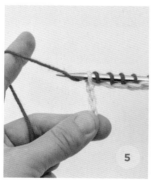

Provisional Cast On

Step 1: Using waste yarn, make a slip knot. Place the slip knot on a crochet hook and hold the crochet hook in your right hand.

Step 2: With your left hand, bring the working yarn over the crochet hook from back to front. Rotate the crochet hook one quarter turn counterclockwise as you hook the working yarn. Draw the hooked yarn through the slip knot. One stitch cast on.

Step 3: Return your crochet hook to its original upward position. In the same manner as the first cast-on stitch, bring the working yarn over the crochet hook from back to front. Hook a loop and draw it through the last cast-on stitch. One stitch cast on.

Repeat Step 3 until you have cast on a few more stitches than called for in the pattern.

Step 4: Break yarn, leaving a 6-inch (15-cm) tail and pull it through the last stitch.

Step 5: Change to your working yarn and knitting needles. Insert your knitting needle into the purl bump side of the crochet chain stitches (not the side of the chain that looks like little "V"s). Pick up the number of stitches called for in the pattern.

Step 6: Continue to work the pattern as described.

Step 7: When you are ready to finish the cast-on edge, pull the tail out of the final crocheted chain stitch. Pull carefully on the waste yarn to undo the chain and place the resulting live knit sts on your knitting needle.

Turkish Cast On

Step 1: Hold your needles parallel in your left hand. The base of your needles will be between your index finger and your thumb, with the tips of your needles pointing away from your hand.

Step 2: Make a slip knot and slide it onto your bottom needle.

Step 3: Hold the tail of your yarn out of the way while you wrap your working yarn around both needles from back to front. Wrap the yarn half as many times as the number of stitches you need to cast on. For example, if you are casting on 50 stitches, you would wrap the yarn 25 times.

Step 4: Pull the bottom needle through so that the top needle and cable are inside the wraps but the bottom needle is free.

Step 5: Use the bottom needle to work across the stitches in the top row according to the pattern.

Step 6: When you reach the end of this first row, turn your work, so that the bottom stitches are on top. The slip knot will be on the top right.

Step 7: Slide the top needle into the stitches and the bottom needle through, so that your top needle and your cable are inside the stitches. Your bottom needle should be free.

Step 8: Drop the slip knot off the needle.

Step 9: Work across the top stitches according to the pattern.

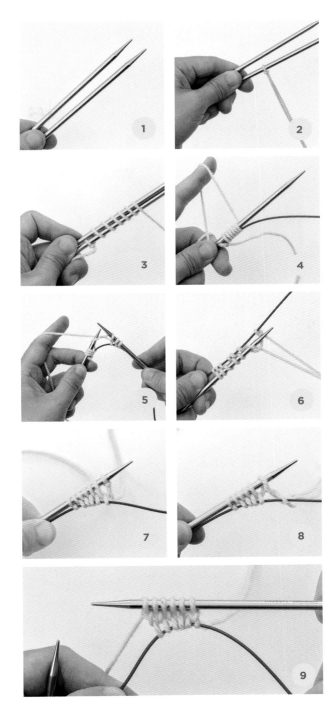

Three-Needle Bind Off

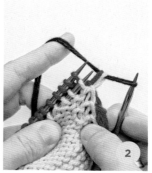

Three-Needle Bind Off

A three-needle bind off is used to join two sets of live stitches. This method of binding off creates a seam with great structure while having the added advantage of being easy to work.

Step 1: Place each set of live stitches on a separate needle in your left hand. For an internal seam, place the wrong sides of your work together. For an external seam, place the right sides of your work together.

Step 2: Using a third needle, insert it knitwise into the first stitch on both the first and second needles and knit the two stitches together.

Step 3: Repeat Step 2. There will be two stitches on your right-hand needle.

Step 4: Using one of your left-hand needles, lift the first stitch on the right-hand needle over the second stitch and off the needle as you normally would when binding off.

Repeat Steps 3 and 4 until one stitch remains on your right-hand needle.

Step 5: Break the yarn, leaving a 6-inch (15-cm) tail. Pull the tail through the last stitch.

Increases & Decreases

cdd (central double decrease)

Slip the two stitches together as if to knit. Knit the next stitch. Pass the slipped stitches over the knit stitch. Two stitches decreased.

K2tog (knit two together, right leaning decrease)

Insert the right-hand needle into the front loops of the first two stitches, from left to right. Knit the two stitches together. One stitch decreased.

M1L (make one left-leaning increase)

Using the left-hand needle, lift the bar between the stitch just worked and the next stitch, from front to back. Knit through the back of the picked-up stitch with the right-hand needle. One stitch increased.

M1R (make one right-leaning increase)

Using the left-hand needle, lift the bar between the stitch just worked and the next stitch, from back to front. Knit through the front of the picked-up stitch with the right-hand needle. One stitch increased.

M1L Purlwise (make one left-leaning increase purlwise, on the wrong side of the work)

Using the left-hand needle, lift the bar between the stitch just worked and the next stitch, from front to back. Purl through the back of the picked-up stitch with the right-hand needle. One stitch increased.

M1R Purlwise (make one right-leaning increase purlwise, on the wrong side of the work)

Using the left-hand needle, lift the bar between the stitch just worked and the next stitch, from back to front. Purl through the front of the picked-up stitch with the right-hand needle. One stitch increased.

ssk (slip, slip, knit, left-leaning decrease)

Slip the first stitch as if to knit. Slip the second stitch as if to knit. Insert the left-hand needle into the front loops of the two slipped stitches, from left to right. Knit the two slipped stitches together. One stitch decreased.

ssp (slip, slip, purl, left-leaning decrease)

Slip the first stitch as if to knit. Slip the second stitch as if to knit. Return both stitches to the left needle in their new orientation. Purl both stitches together through the back loops. One stitch decreased.

Seaming & Grafting

Kitchener Stitch

The Kitchener Stitch is used to join two sets of live stitches without a visible seam. This method is also often referred to as grafting. The Kitchener Stitch lacks the structure of the three-needle bind off but is wonderful for smaller joins that do not support weight in your garment.

To work the Kitchener Stitch, place each set of live stitches on a separate needle in your left hand. Place the wrong sides of your work together. Cut your working yarn so that it is approximately three times the length of the edge you plan to join. Place your working yarn on a blunt tapestry needle.

> Note: When working the following steps, pull the yarn gently. Do not pull the yarn tight or your seam will pucker. It is better to create large loose stitches and adjust the tension at the end of the process than try to loosen tight stitches.

Kitchener Stitch

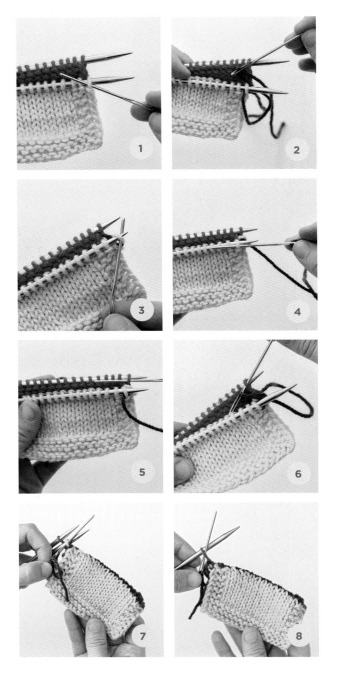

Step 1: Insert the tapestry needle purlwise through the first stitch on the front needle. Pull the yarn through, but do not remove the stitch from the needle.

Step 2: Insert the tapestry needle knitwise through the first stitch on the back needle. Pull the yarn through, but do not remove the stitch from the needle.

Step 3: Insert the tapestry needle knitwise through the first stitch on the front needle. Slip the stitch from the needle and pull the yarn through.

Step 4: Insert the tapestry needle purlwise through the second stitch on the front needle. Pull the yarn through, but do not remove the stitch from the needle.

Step 5: Insert the tapestry needle purlwise through the first stitch on the back needle. Slip the stitch from the needle and pull the yarn through.

Step 6: Insert the tapestry needle knitwise through the second stitch on the back needle. Pull the yarn through, but do not remove the stitch from the needle.

Repeat Steps 3 to 6 until the yarn has been threaded through the last stitch of both the front and back needles.

Step 7: Insert the tapestry needle knitwise through the last stitch on the front needle. Slip the stitch from the needle and pull the yarn through.

Step 8: Insert the tapestry needle knitwise through the last stitch on the back needle. Slip the stitch from the needle and pull the yarn through.

Break the yarn, leaving a 6-inch (15-cm) tail. Adjust the tension of the Kitchener Stitches to match your knitting. Weave in the tail on the wrong side of your work.

Mattress Stitch

The Mattress Stitch is a finishing technique for invisible, vertical seaming.

Step 1: Place the two pieces to be joined side by side. Place a piece of yarn about three times the length you wish to sew on a tapestry needle. Begin at the bottom edge.

Step 2: Bring the tapestry needle from the back to the front of your work at the location where you wish to begin your seam.

Step 3: Bring the needle under one bar between the edge stitches at the bottom of the second knit piece.

Step 4: Insert the needle under the next two bars of the first knit piece, just above your last insertion point.

Step 5: Insert the needle under the next two bars of the second knit piece, just above your last insertion point.

Repeat Steps 4 and 5, alternating sides until the seam is complete. Every few rows, adjust the tension of your seam to match your knitting. Keep in mind that if you overtighten your seam, the seam will pucker.

Tip: When seaming two pieces of self-striping knitting, your stripes may not line up identically. There is no such thing as perfectly matched stripes. You are not a machine, after all, and uniformity is not the ultimate goal. Handmade objects are full of whimsy and irregularities, so don't stress trying to get every stripe to line up perfectly. However, if you find that your stripes very nearly match up on the seam and you want to help them along, here is a fun tip: Instead of picking up two bars on the edge side of your knitting, try picking up one bar or three. Gently tighten the seam to check the look of your stripes, and don't be afraid to rip the seam back a little if you are unhappy with it.

Short Rows

German Short Rows

Work the number of stitches according to the pattern, turn your work, bring the yarn to the front and slip the first stitch as if to purl. Bring the yarn over the needle to the back of your work and pull tight. This will create a double stitch, or DS.

To resolve the double stitch on the following knit or purl row, treat the double stitch as a single stitch. If the double stitch is meant to be a KNIT stitch, knit through BOTH legs of the double stitch as if it were a single stitch. If the double stitch is meant to be a PURL stitch, purl through BOTH legs of the double stitch as if it were a single stitch.

Wrap & Turn Short Rows

On the knit side: Work the number of stitches according to the pattern. Slip the next stitch purlwise. Bring the yarn to the front. Slip stitch from the right-hand needle back to the left-hand needle. Bring the yarn to the back. Turn the work so the purl side is facing you.

On the purl side: Work the number of stitches according to the pattern. Slip the next stitch purlwise. Bring the yarn to the back. Slip stitch from the right-hand needle back to the left-hand needle. Bring the yarn to the front. Turn the work so the knit side is facing you.

To resolve the wrapped stitch, work to the wrapped stitch. For a knit stitch, pick up the wrapped stitch from front to back. For a purl stitch, pick up the wrap from back to front. Place the wrap on the left-hand needle. Work the stitch together with the wrap.

Other Techniques

Dip Left

Bring your yarn to the back of your work. Locate the center stitch in the column of 3 knit stitches on your left-hand needle. Count down four rows. Insert your right-hand needle into the hole at the center of this stitch, from front to back. Wrap your yarn as if to knit. Draw a loop through and leave it on your right-hand needle.

Dip Right

Find the same hole that you pulled your first loop through (when working the Dip Left). Insert your right-hand needle into the center of this stitch from front to back. Wrap your yarn as if to knit. Draw a loop through and leave it on your right-hand needle.

I-Cord

Pick up or cast on the number of stitches called for in the pattern. *Knit all stitches. Slide the stitches from one end of your needle to the other, without turning your work. Repeat from * until you reach your desired length. Bind off all stitches.

LT (left twist)

Knit the second stitch on the left-hand needle through the back loop. Do not remove the stitch from the left-hand needle. Knit the first and second stitches together through the back loops. Slide both stitches off the left-hand needle.

RT (right twist)

Knit two together. Do not remove the stitches from the left-hand needle. Knit into the first stitch just worked, knitwise. Slide both stitches off the left-hand needle.

Yarn Resources

Bad Amy Knits
www.etsy.com/shop/BadAmyKnits

Biscotte Yarns
www.biscotteyarns.com

Canon Hand Dyes
www.canonhanddyes.com

Fab Funky Fibres
www.etsy.com/shop/FabFunkyFibres

Fibernymph Dye Works
www.fibernymphdyeworks.com

Gauge Dye Works
www.gaugedyeworks.com

Kirby Wirby Yarns
www.etsy.com/shop/KirbywirbyYarns

Knitterly Things
www.knitterlythings.com

Leading Men Fiber Arts
www.leadingmenfiberarts.com

Lollipop Yarn
www.lollipopyarnshop.com

Lolodidit
www.lolodidit.com

Mudpunch
www.mudpunch.com

Must Stash Yarn
www.muststashshop.com

Nomadic Yarns
www.nomadicyarns.com

Quaere Fibre
www.quaerefibre.com

The Lemonade Shop
www.thelemonadeshopyarns.com

Third Vault Yarns
www.thirdvaultyarns.com

Turtlepurl Yarns
www.etsy.com/shop/turtlepurl

Valkyrie Fibers
www.etsy.com/shop/ValkyrieFibersTahoe

White Birch Fiber Arts
www.whitebirchfiberarts.com

Acknowledgments

Thank you to all of my knitters who help bring joy to my designs with their constant enthusiasm and imagination. That joy was the fuel for this book.

I am so grateful to the yarn companies that provided yarn support and endless inspiration for the designs in this book. Thank you, Biscotte Yarns, Bad Amy Knits, Canon Hand Dyes, Fab Funky Fibres, Fibernymph Dye Works, Gauge Dye Works, Kirby Wirby Yarns, Knitterly Things, Leading Men Fiber Arts, Lollipop Yarn, Lolodidit, Mudpunch, Must Stash Yarn, Nomadic Yarns, Quaere Fibre, The Lemonade Shop, Valkyrie Fibers, Turtlepurl Yarns and White Birch Fiber Arts.

A HUGE thank you to my incredible, talented and tireless testers for making this book more clear, accurate and fun to knit. Thank you to Kalliopi Aronis, Marissa Austin, Cabe Berg, Marie Biswell, Rosalie Boyle, Amanda Bradley, Joy Bulger, Joy Burkart, Lydia Carlsgaard, Kara Chickering, Heather Cohen, Hope Cooner, Carolyn Crisp, Adrianna Davis, Michelle M. Dolan, Isabell Dröse, Eireen Elliott, Prisca Etzold-Amling, Alison Fisher, Becca Fletcher, Jennifer Gee Conway, Hélène Gomez, Emily Half, Raelene Hall, Renee Hall, Rachel Heim, Lynn Hensley, Katja Hjertaas, Aimee Hubbard, Anna Jones, Nadia K., Mary Kelley, knitter56789, Ashley Kullman, Julie Laffoon, Laura Lambert, Bettina Leclaire, Lisa Mazzitelli, Cheryl McDermott, Shannon Miller, Kara Miltsch, Vicki Norman, Jessica Marie Oliveira, Lauren Palmer-Merrill, Leigh Ann Parente, Alix Paschkowiak, Roberta Pascuzzi, Linda Petre, Élodie Pruneau-Bergeron, Paulina Ramirez, Sarah Reilly, Alicia Rosales, Julie Ross, Lisa K. Ross, Elżbieta Rybicka, Amy Schulze, Suzanne Selby, Tsvetelina Shopova, Deborah Simon, Kathy Simpson, Karrie Snider, Marilyn Stirling, Diane Sullivan, Marta Svobodová, Su Yan Tay, Darcy Thompson, Dawn Umemoto, Joyce Vally, Leah Villa, Stacy Washington, Jackie Whyte, Nicole Williams, Kim Winslow and Diane Zongker.

Thank you to Kanesha Carr, Gytel Lotven, Valdea Lotven, and Sui Hnem Par for making these garments come alive.

Thank you to my sample knitters, Amanda Bradley, Claire Crooke, Rachel Heim and Tricia Rathke, for their hard work and quick hands.

Thank you to my tech editor, Cathy Susko, who is so diligent and committed to helping me craft the best possible patterns.

Thank you to Page Street Publishing and my editor, Rebecca Fofonoff, for making this book possible with their guidance and support. I am thrilled to join their family of authors!

Thank you to my girls for providing regular hug breaks while I knit and designed the patterns in this book. Telly and Dea, you bring me constant inspiration and the best possible support.

Most of all, thank you to my husband, who deserves a vacation when this book is complete. His support of me, my dreams and our family is staggering. I'm constantly in awe of my own good luck at finding such a partner.

About the Author

Stephanie Lotven is an independent knitwear designer whose whimsical knitwear designs have captured the imagination of knitters around the globe. Her work has been featured in collections for Miss Babs Hand-Dyed Yarns, *Harry Potter: Knitting Magic* and *Star Wars: Knitting the Galaxy*. You can find her tutorials, knitting patterns and pattern support on tellybeanknits.com. She lives in Indiana with her exceptionally patient husband and two rowdy daughters. *Knit Happy with Self-Striping Yarn* is her first book.

Index